BIRTH
OF A
NATIONAL
PARK

—◆—

IN THE
GREAT
SMOKY
MOUNTAINS

BIRTH
OF A
NATIONAL
PARK

———•———

IN THE
GREAT
SMOKY
MOUNTAINS

CARLOS C. CAMPBELL

With a Foreword by
HORACE M. ALBRIGHT

Foreword 2009 by
DAVID DALE DICKEY

The University of Tennessee Press
Knoxville

Cloth: first printing, 1960; second printing, revised, 1969; third printing, 1978; fourth printing, 1984.
Paper: first printing, 1993; second printing, 2005; third printing, 2009.

Library of Congress Catalog Card 60-12223

ISBN 13: 978-0-87049-815-2 (paperback: acid-free paper)
ISBN 10: 0-87049-815-0 (paperback: acid-free paper)

TO IDA, my wife, without whose patience and sacrifices
I could not have collected the material for this book.

C.C.C.

CONTENTS

FIGURES

MAPS

FOREWORD 2009

It's so easy to assume that this great National Park, straddling the mountains of Tennessee and North Carolina, was created from lands already owned by the federal government. But that is not the case.

Thousands of citizens, including school children, *bought* the land and *gave* it to the government.

That fact is so little known by the millions who visit the Park today that this historical account, *Birth of a National Park in the Great Smoky Mountains,* is being reissued for the Park's seventy-fifth anniversary, in the year 2009. It was commissioned originally by Great Smoky Mountains Conservation Association in 1960.

The Association was formed in 1923 by individuals in Knoxville, Tennessee, who believed that these mountains, remote and hardly known at the time, warranted permanent protection of their multiple scenic and scientific assets.

But thousands of acres would have to be bought from hundreds of mountain people, from timber companies and mining operations. Where was the money to come from?

This book tells how it was raised by private citizens, officials of towns and cities, and by the states of Tennessee and North Carolina.

After years of effort the Park became a reality, due mainly to unending work by this Association, with help from many dedicated individuals in both states.

Organized to establish the Park "and to protect and promote its interest before and after completion," the Association remains an active voice in Park matters today. It is a nonprofit entity, based in Knoxville, governed by a board of directors of up to twenty-five members.

DAVID DALE DICKEY, Vice-President
For the entire Board of Directors
Great Smoky Mountains Conservation Association

FOREWORD

This was a fine book when first published seventeen years ago. Now in its updated form, it emphasizes even more the wisdom of those far-sighted individuals and groups who helped create the Great Smoky Mountains National Park. For it can be seen here that the visitors who seek the attractions of the Smokies do so in ever-increasing numbers and that, despite the creation of additional national parks, the Great Smoky Mountains National Park continue to outdraw all others. It is appropriate that this dramatic story of the Park's beginnings and development be perpetuated.

The Park lies in a magnificent range, the summit of which is the boundary between North Carolina and Tennessee. One of the largest of the thirty-seven superb reserves comprising our National Park System, it is a region of high mountains, deep valleys, great forests, wildflowers, and shrubs in wide variety and vast profusion. It is in part almost untouched wilderness; in past accessible by good highways and trails. More than eight million visits to the Park were recorded in 1976.

Fifty years ago this outstanding mountain range was known to but a few hardy men and women of the two states in which it lies. Photographs of its natural features were rare. Little had been written about these features except by scientists who had penetrated the remote solitudes of the steep ravines and scaled the peaks of the range. Yet the foothills contained farms and families which had been there for generations, and the paper industry in its quest for reserves of timber had not only acquired large holdings but in some watersheds was beginning to cut and remove the forest which were the last large stands of virgin Southern conifers and hardwoods.

It is fortunate for America that far-seeing men of ideals and great civic pride undertook to save this beautiful mountain paradise. Many individuals contributed time, effort, and personal funds to the planning of this great park project and to the terribly difficult task of carrying it through to completion in the face of disheartening disappointments of such magnitude as to crush lesser people.

The unique movement was launched by W. P. Davis of Knoxville, Tennessee, following a suggestion from Mrs. Davis. The leaders who were largely responsible for the ultimate success of the project were two men of extraordinary foresight, courage and tenacity—Colonel David C. Chapman of Knoxville, Tennessee, and State Senator Mark Squires of Lenoir, North Carolina. These men literally gave their lives to the task of creating the Great Smoky Mountains National Park. They rank with the leaders in the early movements to lay the foundations of the National Parks System—N. P. Langford of Yellowstone, John Muir of Yosemite, Will Steel of Crater Lake, George Stewart of Sequoia, and others who are immortal in the annals of conservation.

Carlos C. Campbell, the author of this book, was in the midst of the long struggle to create the Great Smoky Mountains National Park. He is still active in local organizations supporting the park and the National Park Service. He was on hand when each vital move was made in the long fight against the unbelievable obstacles that apathy, jealousy, political chicanery, and selfishness can bring to bear on a noble project. He has written a clear, accurate, unbiased account of the chain of event in both North Carolina and Tennessee that led to the establishment of the great park, and in so doing has contributed a volume of history significant and valuable in natural resource conservation.

HORACE M. ALBRIGHT
Former Director
National Park Service

INTRODUCTION

ONE OF OUR most persistent tendencies, perhaps, is that of taking things for granted.

Birth of a National Park in the Great Smoky Mountains was written with the hope that some of those people who find inspiration in their visits to the Great Smoky Mountains National Park may not take this park for granted. It did not just happen, as you will see. It was bought with a very large sum of hard-to-get money and a prodigious amount of work in overcoming an amazing number of obstacles.

The material for this history was collected over a period of more than three decades, much of it by personal observation. Memory retained the general picture, but not the details. Such matters as exact amounts of money and acreages had to be checked to refresh the memory and for particulars. Three large scrapbooks, in which most of the progress of the park movement was recorded from day to day, were the principal sources for verification of details and results. One of these was compiled by the East Tennessee Automobile Club and its predecessor, the Knoxville Automobile Club, and the other two by the Great Smoky Mountains Conservation Association. All three were presented years ago to the park to be put in its park-history museum. Microfilms of daily newspapers, available at the Lawson McGhee unit of Knoxville's public library, filled in some of the gaps not covered in the scrapbooks. Minutes of meetings, a great number of letters, and other documents were also used in the process of verification.

Photographs, other than the portraits, which are not otherwise credited were made by the author.

This history was written at the request of officers and directors of the Conservation Association. They desired that all important details of the movement, with interpretations, should be recorded.

The reader will see a surprising number of statements to the effect that, if such and such had not happened, "it might have killed" or "it would have killed" the park movement. That is by no means a matter of crying "Wolf! Wolf!" There were at least a dozen points at which a different turn of events might have been fatal. Certain details concerning these events are, perchance, unpleasant. But the reader who finds the recounting of them a bit labored has the immense advantage of knowing the happy outcome. The park leaders had no such knowledge; they simply faced the unpleasant realities and hoped for that outcome.

Time has justified the hard work and sacrifices of those leaders. And the value of this park to mankind is important enough for that work and those sacrifices. Continuing proof of that statement may be found in the ever-increasing visits to the Great Smokies. Even during the interim between publication of the first edition of this book in 1960 and this revision in 1977, visits grew from 2,000,000 a year to 8,000,000. Meanwhile, the federal government was also creating additional national parks—the twenty-nine parks in 1960 had increased to thirty-seven in 1976.

Hearty thanks are hereby extended to Horace M. Albright, Paul M. Fink, David Dale Dickey, Dr. James T. Tanner, and the others who read the manuscript and made helpful suggestions.

It is only fair to Mr. Albright to explain that several references to him were purposely omitted from the manuscript copy which he read and upon which his introduction was based. These statements were temporarily withheld from Mr. Albright and inserted later, so that he would not see them until after publication.

It is the hope of the author that the people of North Carolina and Tennessee, and visitors from other states and nations, will know and appreciate the fact that this park was purchased at a very high price in money and devoted effort, and that they will strive to protect and preserve its natural beauty for the full enjoyment and inspiration of future generations.

C. C. C.

CHAPTER I

BACKGROUND

THIS IS an account of the unusual movement which led to the establishment of the Great Smoky Mountains National Park in North Carolina and Tennessee. That story can be more easily evaluated, however, if we first take a quick look at national parks as a whole to see how some of the other parks were created and something of their great importance to the people of the United States.

Our National Parks System constitutes one of the nation's major cultural forces. Containing the country's superlative examples of scenic grandeur and some of the outstanding botanical, geological, and historic areas, these parks provide education, relaxation, and inspiration for increasingly large numbers of people.

The volume of more than 250,000,000 visits each year has created a relatively new form of big business. This growing stream of tourists, showing a continuing upward trend, provides the very lifeblood for a large number of cities and communitites. Approximately $100,000,000 yearly is being spent in developing these federal reservations so that they may be enjoyed without damage to their primeval character. Other millions are spent each year for administering and protecting them. Thus, our national parks and related reservations have both aesthetic and economic values in a large measure.

The Great Smoky Mountains National Park is one of the thirty-seven national parks established by Congress and administered by the National Park Service, a bureau of the Department of the Interior. In the beginning, however, there was no central agency to direct and supervise the various units. Each national park was "on

I

its own." Each did its own management and development planning, and each sought its own Congressional financing, or did without.

Yellowstone, mostly in Wyoming but also partly in Montana and Idaho, was the earliest of all national parks, having been created as far back as 1872. It was not only the first national park in the United States but the first in the whole world. In 1870 a group of pioneers, all wilderness-loving men, made an exploring trip into the rugged Yellowstone country to see and learn more regarding a mysterious region about which little was known. Before leaving the mountains and while seated around a campfire on September 19, 1870, they discussed the possibility of private commercial development of the region, which they regarded as likely to become a great future attraction for visitors from all over the area. After considerable discussion, in which Judge Cornelius Hedges, of Helena, Montana, advanced the national park idea, it was decided that the region was so magnificent that it should be preserved and developed for the enjoyment of the whole public throughout the years to come rather than be exploited for the benefit of relatively few private owners. The result was the establishment of Yellowstone National Park, largely through the efforts of N. P. Langford, another member of the exploring expedition. Mr. Langford was the first Yellowstone superintendent, and worked for five years without pay! During that five years he spent much time urging the establishment of other national parks, in addition to handling the multitudinous details incident to administering his own Yellowstone National Park. Because of his boundless zeal for such projects and because of his initials, his friends soon began to refer to him as "National Park" Langford.

Even with the success of the Yellowstone project, there was no other national park until 1890, when three more were created in rapid succession. These were Sequoia, General Grant, and Yosemite, all in California. General Grant National Park was later made a part of the larger Kings Canyon National Park. Although Yosemite did not become a national park until 1890, California established Yosemite Valley as a state park back in 1864, at which time the federal government, through an act of Congress signed by President Abraham Lincoln, gave the valley to the state. The famous landscape architect, Frederick Law Olmsted, Sr., strongly influenced the early preservation of Yosemite Valley. The much larger national park, surrounding but not including the valley, was established in 1890, as stated. In 1906 California gave back the valley to the federal government to become the most important part of Yosemite National Park.

Although the lands for these pioneer national parks and the several that followed in the next few years already belonged to the federal government and merely had to be set aside by Congress, the

3

process was not quite so easy or simple as may appear. The conservation idea, as applied noncommercially (to scenic grandeur, virgin forests, historic shrines, and turbulent rivers), was not generally accepted. Many hurdles had to be cleared, and with little organized support at the beginning. In fact, for some time after they were established the only conservation that was effective in the early national parks came from the "protection" of cavalry troops under a law enacted in 1883.

With only thirteen national parks then established, the Congressional act authorizing the creation of the National Park Service was passed and signed by President Woodrow Wilson on August 25, 1916. Unfortunately, however, there was no appropriation to defray even the meager expenses until the following April. Meantime, in February, 1917, Mt. McKinley National Park, in Alaska, was authorized.

The first director of the newly created National Park Service was Stephen T. Mather, who for more than two years had been assistant to the Secretary of the Interior. Horace M. Albright was named as assistant director. Their appointments were made by Franklin K. Lane, the conservation-minded Secretary of the Interior. As Mr. Albright recalled in a published article: "Secretary Lane, Mr. Mather and I were conservationists of the Theodore Roosevelt school." [1]

In that article Albright, who succeeded Mather in 1929, included a summary of major problems which were encountered during the early years of the National Park Service:

Troubles came thick and fast. The most serious problems arose from the excitement of the War [World War I] and the greedy ... profiteers. Sheep and cattle men sought to graze their herds in the great parks of the West, and for a while there was insistent demand to kill the elk of the Yellowstone country for meat for the soldiers! ...

I recall that one morning soon after we entered the War, Secretary Lane showed me a telegram from the President of the University of California, his and Mr. Mather's and my Alma Mater. President Benjamin Ide Wheeler, as head of the California Council of National Defense, demanded

[1] Horace M. Albright, "The National Park Service, 1917–1937," reprinted from *American Planning and Civic Annual,* 1937, p. 48.

4

permission to send 50,000 head of sheep into Yosemite National Park. It required strenuous efforts to build a counteroffensive against my college president through California friends of the Parks, mainly the Sierra Club.

In the state of Washington, only the dramatic demand of the Mountaineers of Tacoma and Seattle that their lawns and golf courses be grazed before sacrificing the wild flower gardens of Mt. Rainier saved these virgin meadows and slopes of the Park....

No one not connected with the struggle to build up this national park system can imagine the difficulties that had to be overcome to secure new parks or enlarge old ones. Almost every local grazing, irrigation, power, timber and resort interest, directly or indirectly affected, opposed us. Counties feared the loss of taxable property and held up our projects. Another Government bureau not only withheld support but organized local commercial interests against us. It took ten years to add Kern River Canyon and Mt. Whitney to Sequoia National Park, and thirteen years to get a partial Grand Teton National Park....

After the Armistice ... came a demand for more homesteads on the public domain of the West, and this promoted irrigation projects which threatened the Yellowstone and other national parks with more serious exploitation than grazing sheep would have wrought in war time. The fights against irrigation reservoirs and related works occupied much [of the park men's] time for two years, but in the end, with the aid of strong outside organizations, we were successful in defeating all such projects submitted.

We had some bitter personal enemies to combat. It was necessary to bring legal action against Ralph H. Cameron of Arizona to eject him from mining claims controlling strategic points and trail routes in the Grand Canyon. Just as the U. S. Supreme Court ordered his removal, he was elected U. S. Senator. For years, he fought the Park Service in season and out. He and Senator [Robert N.] Stanfield of Oregon, who disliked the Forest Service, got a Senate Resolution approved directing an investigation of both Services. A very unfair inquiry kept our organizations in turmoil most of 1925. It ended disastrously for both senators, as both were defeated in 1926, but before leaving the Senate, Mr. Cameron was forced out of the Grand Canyon under threat of punishment for contempt of the Supreme Court.[2]

[2] *Ibid.*, 49–53, *passim.*

Mr. Albright credits Congressman Louis C. Cramton, of Michigan, as being an exceptionally effective early supporter of the national parks program in Congress. Cramton, who served for ten years as chairman of the Department of the Interior subcommittee of the House Appropriations Committee, helped to build a sound financial structure for the National Park Service. He assisted Secretary Lane and Mr. Mather in charting a course for a sane development program in which the primeval and historic aspects of various parks would be given maximum protection. He was the principal spokesman for the Park Service on the floor of the House of Representatives. In one speech, in which he was discussing Mr. Mather's achievements, he said: "There will never come an end to the good that he has done."

Mr. Albright insists that Cramton's name be linked with that of Mather in relating the story of the formative years of the National Park Service. Obviously a third name, Albright, should also be included.

As already shown, it was extremely difficult to establish a national park even when the federal government already owned the land. A new and even more vexing chapter in the national parks story was soon to be written, however. Near the end of 1923 and on into 1924 a movement was launched to establish a national park where all of the land was in private ownership—the Great Smoky Mountains National Park. Problems not experienced in the creation of the first seventeen national parks were to plague the new project.

It was no easy matter to convince the National Park Service that the then relatively unknown area in North Carolina and Tennessee was worthy of admission into such select company because many other areas, some of which were then better known, were also clamoring for recognition. And at times it seemed utterly impossible to raise the estimated $10,000,000 needed for purchase money. Furthermore, the high praise heaped on the area in the effort to make it seem suitable for acceptance and to raise the necessary money served to make the acquisition of land much more difficult and more expensive than had been expected.

Three more national parks were added to the chain before the Great Smoky Mountains National Park was officially completed and thus became the twenty-second park. Since that time, the Park

6

System has continued to develop, so that by 1976 it embraced a total of thirty-seven national parks.

Chonological Order of Establishment

It is understandable that differences of opinion exist as to the actual dates of "establishment" of several of the parks because these parks were the result of different official steps, not just one single action. In some instances there would be an act of Congress authorizing the establishment. Then in due course of time the area would be accepted "for protection and administration" only. In certain cases, as in the Great Smokies, there was a final act of Congress stating that the area was then authorized "for full development." In several other instances, also, the national parks had previously been national monuments or some other type of federal reservation.

Establishment dates used in the following chronological list are those after which full development was permitted, as shown in the government publication *Areas Administered by the National Park Service*.[3] The thirty-seven parks, with their respective dates of official establishment and the states in which they are located, are as follows:

1872—Yellowstone, in Wyoming, Montana, and Idaho
1890—Sequoia, in California
1890—Yosemite, in California
1890—General Grant, in California (absorbed by Kings Canyon in 1940)
1899—Mt. Rainier, in Washington
1902—Crater Lake, in Oregon
1903—Wind Cave, in South Dakota
1906—Mesa Verde, in Colorado
1910—Glacier, in Montana
1915—Rocky Mountain, in Colorado
1916—Hawaii Volcanoes, in Hawaii

[3] *National Parks & Landmarks*, United States Department of the Interior, National Park Service (Washington, D.C., Government Printing Office, 1968, with an addendum dated February 8, 1977), pp. 4–22.

1916—Lassen Volcanic, in California

   (National Park Service created August 25, 1916, but did not get operating money until April 17, 1917)

1917—Mt. McKinley, in Alaska

1919—Acadia, in Maine (the first in the East)

1919—Grand Canyon, in Arizona

1919—Zion, in Utah

1921—Hot Springs, in Arkansas

   (Great Smokies movement launched in 1923)

1928—Bryce Canyon, in Utah

1929—Grand Teton, in Wyoming

1930—Carlsbad Caverns, in New Mexico

1934—Great Smoky Mountains, in North Carolina and Tennessee

1935—Shenandoah, in Virginia

1938—Olympic, in Washington

1940—Kings Canyon, in California (which absorbed General Grant National Park, created in 1890)

1940—Isle Royale, in Michigan

1941—Mammoth Cave, in Kentucky

1944—Big Bend, in Texas

1947—Everglades, in Florida

1956—Virgin Islands, on St. John Island, Virgin Islands

1961—Haleakala, in Hawaii

1962—Petrified Forest, in Arizona

1964—Canyonlands, in Utah

1966—Guadalupe Mountains, in Texas

1968—North Cascades, in Washington

1968—Redwoods, in California

1971—Voyageurs, in Minnesota

1971—Arches, in Utah

1971—Capitol, in Utah

Platt, in Oklahoma, previously listed as a National Park, has been reclassified and made a part of Chickasaw National Recreation Area.

Although Hot Springs National Park was not given official status until 1921, it had been a federal reservation since 1832. Mesa Verde and Platt National Parks were established on the same day, June 29, 1906. Grand Canyon and Acadia National Parks likewise share a common date, February 26, 1919, Zion National Park being authorized later in the same year. In other instances where two parks were created in the same year the earlier is listed first.

In addition to directing the destinies of these thirty-seven national parks, with over 15,000,000 acres of highly diversified lands, the National Park Service also administers 286 other federal reservations containing more than 29,000,000 additional acres of land. These include national historical parks, national monuments, national military parks, a national memorial park, national battlefield parks, national battlefield sites, national historic sites, national memorials, national cemeteries, a national seashore recreational area, national parkways, and Washington's National Capital Parks. As though this were not enough, it also supervises three non-federal recreational areas which contain over 2,000,000 acres of land. Thus, the National Park Service administers much of the nation's most interesting land for the education, relaxation, and inspiration of the people of the United States and other countries.

Stephen T. Mather, the first director, began his connection with the government in 1915. As assistant to the Secretary of the Interior, his first government position, he had the task of correlating the activities of the various national parks existing at that time, of setting up a method of administering them, and of adding to their number. During more than two years he helped to create the National Park Service. In 1919, Horace M. Albright, the first assistant director, was made superintendent of Yellowstone National Park and Arno B. Cammerer was brought in to succeed him as assistant director. Although both Mather and Albright had planned to return to private life after putting the Service "on its feet," the former remained until after a stroke at the end of 1928 and the latter until his resignation in 1933. The succession of directors of the National Park Service and their periods of service follow:

Directors	Periods of Service
Stephen T. Mather	May 16, 1917—January 8, 1929
Horace M. Albright	January 12, 1929—August 9, 1933
Arno B. Cammerer	August 10, 1933—August 9, 1940
Newton B. Drury	August 20, 1940—March 31, 1951
Arthur E. Demaray	April 1, 1951—December 8, 1951

Conrad L. Wirth	December 9, 1951—January 12, 1964
George B. Hartzog, Jr.	January 13, 1964—January 7, 1973
Ronald Walker	January 8, 1973—January 8, 1975
Gary E. Everhardt	January 9, 1975—May 27, 1977
William J. Whalen	May 28, 1977—

Enjoyment Without Impairment

The national parks are developed so as to permit their use and enjoyment without destroying their original splendor or historic values. Practices and regulations of the National Park Service, based on an act of Congress, are designed "to conserve the scenery and the natural and historic objects and the wildlife therein and to provide for the enjoyment of the same in such a manner and by such means as will leave them unimpaired for the enjoyment of future generations." The Service has done a remarkably good job of harmonizing these two somewhat opposing goals, that of conserving and at the same time using.

Each national park preserves and exibits something that is fine and distinctive. Each is wonderful in its own peculiar way and is a valuable asset that belongs to all the people of America.

Something of the inspirational value of these parks was expressed by J. A. (Cap) Krug, then Secretary of the Interior, as he spoke at the 1946 dedication of Olympic National Park in Washington. Here is a significant part of his message, uttered after a tribute to the early settlers and particularly to those who had helped to establish the first national parks:

Let us not forget that part of the great spirit and broad vision of these pioneers came from the grandeur of the continent itself. The very boldness of their spirit was a reflection of the size and greatness of the land they settled. It is little enough to ask that their children, and grandchildren, and generations yet unborn shall be able, through enjoying National Parks such as these, to know something of the pristine glory of their country. Whatever the future may bring, our descendants will rejoice in this great symbol of the beauty and glory of America.

Many efforts have been made to describe adequately and accurately the charm of various scenic masterpieces of our national parks. Most people who endeavor to paint word-pictures of such glorious spots quickly realize the impossibility of the task. A visitor to Grand Canyon National Park summed it up in this manner: "Nature has put her own descriptions here in the Arizona desert. But her story can only be appreciated in the original. Any effort at translation by word of mouth, through writing or by pictures, is futile."

So it is with each national park. Full enjoyment and appreciation come only through personal experiences on the spot. Who, for instance, can describe a glorious sunrise from Myrtle Point of majestic Mt. Le Conte in the Great Smokies?

One of the main functions of photographs and word-pictures of our national parks is to arouse enough interest and curiosity to encourage the reader to go to see for himself, and thus reap the greater rewards from the personal visit. It is somewhat similar to the summary of a fine play or a drama critic's review of it. Neither the summary nor the review, however good, could ever take the place of the play itself. The parks—like the play—are the real attractions, not what someone has written about them.

It is the hope that every reader of this book can and sometime will explore for himself the Great Smokies and our nation's other superb parks. Only such a person can ever know the full value and significance of our national parks.

CHAPTER 2

THE RESULT OF AN IDEA

HISTORY was made, and a precedent for the creation of future national parks was set in the establishment of the Great Smoky Mountains National Park. Creation of the eighteen national parks prior to 1924 had been accomplished by the setting aside of lands which already belonged to the federal government. Not so with the Great Smokies. The 515,225.8 acres constituting this park were then in private ownership, in more than 6,600 separate tracts. Approximately one-third of this area was still primeval forest. On some of the remaining acreage there had been only selective cutting of timber. Much of the rest was in varying stages of reforestation, after having been cut over by lumber companies or cleared by mountain farmers.

Most—over 85 per cent—of the area was owned by eighteen timber and pulpwood companies. Some 1,200 tracts were farms of various sizes. Worst of all, however, from the land-buying standpoint, was the fact that there were over 5,000 lots and summer homes. It was as difficult to buy some of these tiny plots as it was to get certain of the big holdings of lumber companies. Many of the lots had been "won" several years earlier in a promotional scheme, and it was impossible to locate some of the "owners," who had never even bothered to pay taxes on their lots. A tremendous amount of effort went into getting the necessary legislation and money, and then into surveying, appraising, and buying the land. This part of the project required over ten years of full-scale activity, with several more years of winding up the loose ends.

Prior to the 1923 launching of the successful movement (there had been previous movements and suggestions that were not successful), very few people knew anything about the Great Smoky Mountains. In Knoxville, from whose high ridges and taller buildings the mountain peaks can be seen, the man in the street had only the vaguest of ideas where the Great Smokies were located. The names Le Conte, Clingmans Dome, Thunderhead and Gregory Bald he had never even heard.

Most previous references had treated the Smokies as a despised barrier between Knoxville and western North Carolina. Since Knoxville was an active wholesale and manufacturing center, businessmen longed for the day when they could have easier access to the trade territory just across the mountains. If they had possessed the power to do so, they would have wished these rugged mountains out of existence. A leading topic of discussion at most gatherings of businessmen was ways and means of getting a road to connect eastern Tennessee and western North Carolina.

Various routes for such a road were discussed. Some urged that it be built up the Little Tennessee River. Quite a number favored crossing the main crest at Ekaneetlee Gap, the lowest point in the section of the mountains that rise above Cades Cove. A few suggested crossing at Spence Field, at the west end of Thunderhead. A majority, however, advocated Indian Gap, above Gatlinburg.

Such was the atmosphere in which the successful park movement was born during the latter part of 1923. In the summer of that year Mr. and Mrs. Willis P. Davis, of Knoxville, had made a Western trip, during which they visited some of the national parks. As they feasted their eyes on the dramatic, towering, snow-capped peaks, Mrs. Davis, although admitting that what they were seeing was truly wonderful, insisted that those mountains were not a bit more beautiful than were the green-clad peaks and ridges of the Great Smoky Mountains—only a tiny bit of which they had seen as they rode the logging train to Elkmont.

"Why can't we have a national park in the Great Smokies?" she asked her husband.

Mr. Davis, then manager of Knoxville Iron Company, liked the idea. Immediately after returning to Knoxville he began to tell friends, one and all, about "the wonderful national park we are going to get in the Great Smokies." Despite the fact that the virgin

13

timber had been or was being cut by the Little River Lumber Company, the steeply rising mountains that flank Little River Gorge were fascinatingly beautiful to the Davises. Not only did Mr. Davis believe that the region should be made a national park, so as to save much of the virgin timber, but he urged others to help launch a movement to bring it about.

In retrospect it seems strange that support should have come so slowly. It will be recalled, however, that up to this time the only interest had been to get a commercial road. There had been no mention of the aesthetic values of the proposed road. So most of Mr. Davis' words fell on deaf ears or at least on highly skeptical ears.

A personal reference is given only because it is typical of what Mr. Davis had to contend with during the early stages. As assistant manager, and shortly afterward manager, of the Knoxville Chamber of Commerce, the writer had occasion to confer with him often, for he was a member of the Chamber's board of directors. During those conferences I was often irritated because I had to listen to him "rave"—and that is what I then felt it amounted to—about the superlative beauty of the Great Smokies and the national park that we were to have there. I tried to be courteous. In fact, no one would have wanted to be otherwise to a man who was so innately dignified and gentlemanly. But I was not interested in his visions of a national park, nor were most of the others who "had to listen" to him. Up to that time I just barely knew that the Great Smokies existed. I had heard of Mt. Le Conte, for instance, only through a series of letters in 1921 from Paul M. Fink of Jonesboro, Tennessee, urging that the Chamber of Commerce seek to get a national park on Mt. Le Conte. I had never heard of Chimney Tops, the Jump-Off, Mt. Guyot, Clingmans Dome, Thunderhead, Gregory Bald, Cades Cove and the many other place names that have since become so familiar to so many people throughout the nation.

Several of the men who later became active in the movement, including those who provided most of the later leadership, frankly admitted that at first they regarded Mr. Davis' idea as a big joke, that the most they had dared hope for was to get some good publicity for Knoxville. In fact, for a few months, at least, Mr. and

Mrs. Davis were the only two people who really believed that a national park was a possibility.

Ideas and Movements

For a full understanding of the successful movement and its claim to special recognition, it is important to make a few distinctions and clarifications. Mrs. Davis' conception of a national park was not the first, nor was that of Mr. Fink, to which reference has just been made. Some are convinced that W. M. Goodman had this idea in mind when he promoted the National Conservation Exposition in Knoxville in 1913. The evidence, however, is that, although there was a somewhat nebulous sentiment for a national park at that time, most of the references were to national forests or just plain "conservation." At any rate, neither the Fink nor the Goodman idea ever reached the proportions of a movement.

The only actual previous movement for a national park in the Southern Appalachian Mountains—and it was neither specifically nor exclusively identified with the Great Smokies—was one launched in Asheville, North Carolina, in 1899, after several years of discussion. The Appalachian National Park Association was formed at a two-day meeting. On January 4, 1900, it presented to Congress a memorial containing "all the reasons that anyone could think of" for establishing a national park. It is interesting to note that the Senate Agriculture Committee notified the Association that any action which the federal government might take in the matter would interfere with states' rights, and recommended that the group get official approval of the states involved. Legislatures of six states —North Carolina, South Carolina, Georgia, Alabama, Tennessee and Virginia—gave such approval early in 1901.[1]

Shortly afterward, however, the Association learned that the federal government had already gone on record as opposing the purchase of lands at any time for national park purposes. For this reason the Association changed its name from the Appalachian Na-

---

[1] George A. McCoy, *A Brief History of the Great Smoky Mountains National Park Movement in North Carolina* (Asheville, North Carolina, Inland Press), 1940, pp. 19–23.

tional Park Association to the Appalachian National Forest Reserve Association.[2]

The revised and re-named organization then worked actively for the creation of a national forest rather than a national park, but only after some ten years of work did it see the establishment of the desired forest reserves. In the final victory it had the effective help of the American Forestry Association.[3]

The very fact that the North Carolina group abandoned the fight for a national park and adopted a different and far easier goal must disqualify its efforts as a step in the successful movement that started in 1923. In fact, there is no connection between the Davis movement and any previous project or idea.

For a short time it appeared that the movement started by Mr. Davis might not fare any better—or that it might wind up with a similar change of objective, a national forest rather than a national park. According to the *Knoxville Sentinel* of October 29, 1923, a committee had been appointed by the Chamber of Commerce to work with one from the Knoxville Automobile Club in an effort to get a national park "in the Southern Appalachians" because of the opportunities such an area would give for good scenery, pioneer history, and hunting. No one present then knew that hunting is never permitted in national parks. No further reference to any such committee has been traced.

Although there had been a few informal conferences, the first meeting recorded in the minutes of the Great Smoky Mountains Conservation Association, held in the law offices of Judge H. B. Lindsay on December 21, 1923, elected Mr. Davis as chairman, J. Wylie Brownlee as secretary, and Cowan Rodgers as treasurer. Others attending the meeting were Colonel David C. Chapman, wholesale druggist; and Forrest Andrews, Judge D. C. Webb, James B. Wright, and Judge Lindsay—four attorneys who represented companies which owned large tracts of land in the Smokies. Insofar as the minutes showed, the group did not adopt a name.

At the next recorded meeting a motion to adopt the name Smoky Mountains Park Association was voted down, and the name Smoky

---

[2] *Ibid.*, pp. 24–25.
[3] *Ibid.*, *passim.*

16

Mountain Forest Reserve Association was adopted. At an unrecorded meeting held in the office of the Knoxville Chamber of Commerce, Mr. Davis suggested that the Chamber adopt the park movement as a special project. Manager E. N. Farris objected, indicating that such an ambitious project should be handled by a special organization. It should, perhaps, be explained that at the time Mr. Farris was a sick man, although it was not generally known; he died shortly afterwards.

A similar suggestion made later by Mr. Davis to the directors of the Knoxville Automobile Club (later the East Tennessee Automobile Club) brought somewhat better cooperation, which finally resulted in the forming of the Great Smoky Mountains Conservation Association. Directors of the two organizations were identical, but with different officers. Russell W. Hanlon, then secretary-manager of the "Auto Club," said that it was often difficult to determine which group was meeting. Hanlon succeeded Brownlee as secretary of the Association January 18, 1924.

Association minutes do not show when or how the Forest Reserve name was dropped or changed, or just when the name Great Smoky Mountains Conservation Association was adopted. But, after the change was made, there seems to have been a studied effort to make it known, as is indicated by the fact that in at least one news story the name appeared as Smoky Mountain National Park Association. In those early days the word "Great" was frequently omitted and the "s" was as often omitted in the word "Mountains."

Minutes of meetings and news stories reveal that the desire for a road or roads across the Smokies was at first as eagerly sought as was the park itself. In fact, a news story once reported that the Conservation Association would support the movement for a national park in the Smokies "as well as the road." There was then no road crossing the Southern Appalachians from the French Broad River to the Georgia line, an air distance of approximately one hundred miles which includes much more than the Great Smokies proper.[4]

[4] In view of a rather general tendency of Southern mountain communities far removed from the Great Smokies to refer to their mountains as "Great Smokies," attention is called to the fact that the Board on Geographic Names, Department of the Interior, defines the Great Smokies as that segment of the Unaka range, or state-line

Although Colonel Chapman often remarked that he was not present at the first few conferences, he did attend the "organizational" meeting on December 21, 1923. He admitted, however, that for several weeks he was somewhat less than enthusiastic about any possibility of getting a national park. In fact, he was as skeptical as most of the other "recruits." In reminiscing, he would say that he had hunted and fished all up and down Little River, as he spent much time at the Elkmont summer colony, and that he knew it was beautiful country, but had never dreamed of its being anything unusual or distinctive: "Not until I accidentally saw a copy of President Theodore Roosevelt's report on the Southern Appalachians [5] did I have any idea of just what we have here. In reading and rereading this report I learned for the first time that the Great Smokies have some truly superlative qualities. After that I became keenly interested in Mr. Davis' plan and realized that a national park should be a possibility."

Although Mr. Davis was president of the Conservation Association and its active leader, Colonel Chapman steadily increased the amount and scope of his own work. Because of his new zeal and a great willingness to work he was put more and more in the place of leadership of the movement. Mr. Davis welcomed this new source of power enthusiastically and went so far as to recommend that Chapman be elected president of the group—an honor which the Colonel promptly declined. He was, nevertheless, made chairman of the board and given almost unlimited authority.

Father of the Park?

Colonel Chapman is often referred to as "father" of the park. The genealogy is, however, rather confused. Perhaps the more appropriate term for him is "foster-father," for Mr. and Mrs. Davis should be regarded as the "parents" because they gave birth to the idea and the movement. Further, the park might not have been es-

---

range, lying between the Pigeon River and the Little Tennessee River. This is an airline distance of about fifty miles, but with a meandering crest of seventy-three miles. The park stops short of this extent by approximately a mile at each end.

[5] *Message of the President of the United States, Transmitting a Report of the Secretary of Agriculture in Relation to the Forests, Rivers and Mountains of the Southern Appalachian Region* (Washington, 1902, Government Printing Office).

MT. LE CONTE, showing its many peaks and spurs: It is both the "height of mountain" (6,593 ft.) and the "depth of valley" (1,292 ft. at base in Gatlinburg) that make this the *tallest* mountain in the eastern United States.

—*Jim Thompson*

MARK SQUIRES
Inspired leader in North Carolina

DAVID C. CHAPMAN
Dynamic leader of the movement

tablished at all if Mr. Davis had not possessed certain important qualities—among them his Christian Science faith. His implicit confidence of ultimate success carried the project over some seemingly insurmountable difficulties, especially during the first years. When the outcome was most uncertain, his answer to inquiries was always a cheerful "Everything is going along just fine. We're going to get a national park in the Great Smokies."

This appreciation of Mr. Davis' important contributions to the project in the planning stages does not in any way imply, however, that Colonel Chapman has been given too much credit for his work. That would be hard to do. It is more a matter of terminology. Let it be said that few foster-fathers ever did as much for a foster-child as Colonel Chapman did for this park, guiding it through the troublesome growing period and giving it a real chance in life.

But let us get back to the specific problems incident to establishment of the park. The leaders were soon faced with a serious dilemma. In order to arouse enough interest to get people to subscribe money for promotion and land purchases and to get Congress to accept the area as a national park, the spectacular beauty and scenic grandeur of the region had to be described repeatedly. But to get the land at reasonable prices, the owners had to be shown that their mountain land was relatively worthless for other purposes. The area was presented on the one hand as one of the nation's most wonderful spots, on the other as rugged, practically inaccessible, and, except for its scenic value, worth very little. Without the first part of the description the necessary money could not have been gotten. But, unfortunately, the landowners were hearing that description and were perfectly willing to believe that they owned something almost priceless in value. Even with the later efforts of park leaders to show that much of the land was too rough and too isolated for successful logging and that the foothills farms were relatively unproductive, the owners still clung to their built-up values. It would have taken a good part of the gold in Fort Knox to have bought the necessary land if it had not been for the right of condemnation which was given by the legislatures of the two states.

It is a coincidence, but without actual connection, that, about the same time that Mr. Davis was buttonholing his Knoxville friends

GREAT SMOKY MOUNTAINS

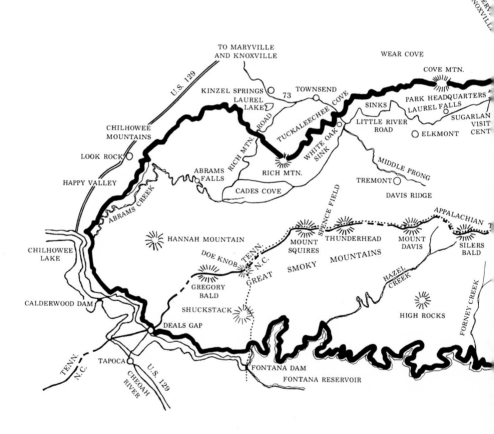

TO MARYVILLE
AND KNOXVILLE

WEAR COVE

COVE MTN.

U.S. 129

KINZEL SPRINGS
LAUREL LAKE

73

TOWNSEND

PARK HEADQUARTERS
LAUREL FALLS

SINKS

SUGARLAN
VISIT
CENT

CHILHOWEE
MOUNTAINS

LITTLE RIVER
ROAD

ELKMONT

LOOK ROCK

RICH MTN. ROAD

TUCKALEECHEE COVE

WHITE OAK SINK

MIDDLE PRONG

ABRAMS
FALLS

RICH MTN.

TREMONT

HAPPY VALLEY

ABRAMS CREEK

CADES COVE

DAVIS RIDGE

APPALACHIAN T

SPENCE FIELD

HANNAH MOUNTAIN

MOUNT
SQUIRES

THUNDERHEAD

MOUNT
DAVIS

SILERS
BALD

CHILHOWEE
LAKE

DOE KNOB

SMOKY MOUNTAINS

HAZEL CREEK

TENN.
N.C.

GREAT

GREGORY
BALD

FORNEY CREEK

CALDERWOOD DAM

SHUCKSTACK

HIGH ROCKS

DEALS GAP

TENN.
N.C.

TAPOCA

U.S. 129

CHEOAH RIVER

FONTANA DAM
FONTANA RESERVOIR

U.S.
TO SEVIER
AND KNOXVILL

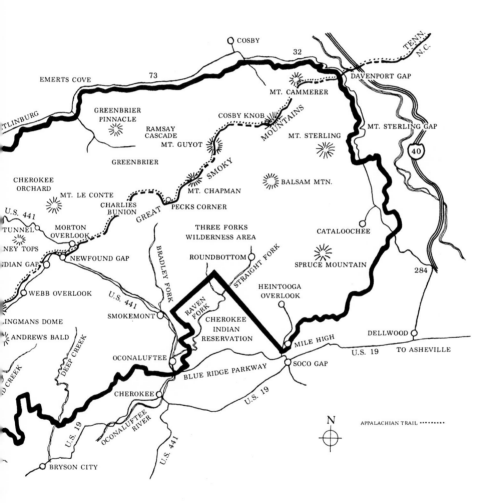

COSBY

32

TENN.
N.C.

EMERTS COVE 73

DAVENPORT GAP

TLINBURG

MT. CAMMERER

GREENBRIER
PINNACLE

COSBY KNOB

MOUNTAINS

MT. STERLING GAP

RAMSAY
CASCADE

MT. STERLING

40

MT. GUYOT

GREENBRIER

SMOKY

CHEROKEE
ORCHARD

BALSAM MTN.

MT. LE CONTE

MT. CHAPMAN

U.S. 441

CHARLIES
BUNION

PECKS CORNER

GREAT

TUNNEL

MORTON
OVERLOOK

THREE FORKS
WILDERNESS AREA

CATALOOCHEE

NEY TOPS

ROUNDBOTTOM

SPRUCE MOUNTAIN

284

DIAN GAP

NEWFOUND GAP

BRADLEY FORK

STRAIGHT FORK

WEBB OVERLOOK

U.S. 441

HEINTOOGA
OVERLOOK

INGMANS DOME

SMOKEMONT

RAVEN
FORK

CHEROKEE
INDIAN
RESERVATION

DELLWOOD

ANDREWS BALD

MILE HIGH

DEEP CREEK

OCONALUFTEE

U.S. 19

TO ASHEVILLE

D CREEK

BLUE RIDGE PARKWAY

SOCO GAP

CHEROKEE

U.S. 19

U.S. 19

OCONALUFTEE
RIVER

N

APPALACHIAN TRAIL ·········

U.S. 441

BRYSON CITY

and talking incessantly about "this wonderful national park" which we were to have in the Great Smokies, there was considerable talk in Washington and several Southern communities about the need for such a park. Stephen T. Mather, the efficient first director of the National Park Service, had recommended that another be established in the East, probably in the Southeast. At the time, Acadia, off the coast of Maine, was the only national park in the East.

Mr. Davis had presented his idea for a Great Smokies park to Dr. Hubert Work, Secretary of the Interior, in the fall of 1923. But the claims of approximately thirty other communities were also advanced for their respective areas shortly after the park talk began to appear more and more often in newspapers throughout the South. This widespread interest led Secretary Work to appoint an unofficial committee of five to investigate as many recommended sites and possible other areas as they could to see if any of them measured up to the high standards already set for national parks.

This committee, known as the Southern Appalachian National Park Committee, was composed of Harlan P. Kelsey, of Massachusetts, representing the Appalachian Mountain Club; William C. Gregg, of New Jersey, representing the American Civic Association; Colonel Glenn S. Smith, of the United States Geological Survey; Congressman H. W. Temple, of Pennsylvania; and Major W. A. Welch, general manager of Palisades Interstate Park, New York and New Jersey. The planned itinerary for the committee's trip of inspection went as far south as northern Georgia and Alabama— but did not even include the Great Smokies. This came as a surprise and sore disappointment to the Conservation Association group, especially since it was known that Mr. Kelsey, a leading member of the committee, was somewhat familiar with the distinctive qualities of the Great Smokies. In fact, in a letter to Paul M. Fink, of Jonesboro, on November 15, 1923, he wrote regarding the question of a site: "It occurs to me that the region around Mount Guyot, Le Conte and Clingmans Dome appears to be the wildest and best beginning for such a park."

In the same letter Kelsey asked for ideas on a Southern Appalachian National Park, requesting that Fink let him know what he found the feeling in the South to be on national park matters and what he thought would be the best center.

In view of Fink's enthusiastic recommendation of the Great Smokies, it is wondered if the omission of this area leads to the possible explanation that the itinerary may have been formulated in Washington without consulting members of the committee.

At this time Colonel Chapman joined Mr. Davis in repeating the request of 1923 for establishment of the park in the Smokies, and efforts were made to get the committee to alter its course as it worked back northward—but to no avail. It would not come to Knoxville, and only with reluctance did it even agree to give our representatives a hearing in Asheville, where the committee was to start its study of the Grandfather Mountain-Linville Gorge area.

Conservation Association workers accepted the "invitation" to go to Asheville, for it appeared to be their only chance to present their cause to the investigating committee. This they did on July 30, 1924. Asheville was, of course, in "hostile" territory. Asheville and surrounding sections of North Carolina were not only pushing the Grandfather Mountain-Linville Gorge site, but in connection with it were actively working against a possible selection of the Great Smokies.

It was, therefore, a fighting delegation that represented the cause of the Great Smokies at the Asheville meeting. In the group, besides Davis, Chapman, and Fink, were Congressman J. Will Taylor, General Frank Maloney, Forrest Andrews, Russell W. Hanlon, and I. W. Rawlings. At that early stage of the movement only three members of the delegation—Andrews, Fink, and Maloney—had a general firsthand knowledge of the whole proposed area. Information of others was limited to the Little River Gorge and Elkmont areas, their enthusiasm for other sections being based largely upon what they had heard.

Pictures Prove Effective

Remembering the old Chinese proverb, "A picture is worth more than 10,000 words," the Conservation Association early in the movement had designated James E. (Jim) Thompson as its official photographer. Pictures of rare beauty were supplied in great abundance by Mr. Thompson, who was a Great Smokies enthusiast. He went into remote sections of the area and brought back pictorial evidence of the charm and majesty that was later to be enjoyed firsthand by millions of people. The words "remote sections" are used in the light of what is now known of the Smokies. In those days most sections of the park area were indeed "remote." Not merely were the Thompson pictures used as powerful aids in those early days, but their use and value—and the infinite variety of subject matter—grew with the park movement. It requires no stretch of one's imagination to realize that without the help of these magnificent views there might have been no national park in the Great Smokies.

CHAPTER 3

THE GREAT SMOKIES
RECOMMENDED

REGARDING the subject of the meeting in Asheville, it is true that enlargements of numerous pictures had a particularly important part in catching the active interest of at least two of the five members of Secretary Work's committee. After a three-hour meeting, Kelsey and Gregg decided to take a personal look in the near future.

This they did. On August 6, 1924, they climbed majestic Mt. Le Conte. Prior to the trip the Association had made elaborate plans. A crew of workmen had cleared a "trail" up the creek by way of the now-famous Rainbow Falls. Actually it by no means rated the name of trail, for nothing more than some of the underbrush and the worst windfalls had been removed so that the climbers could find their way over or around the boulder-strewn route. Even so, the trail-clearing represented a tremendous lot of work.

The trip was an eye-opener! The sheer ruggedness of the trailside was most impressive. The primitive beauty of the virgin forests—mixed hardwoods in the lower and intermediate elevations, and red spruce and fir (or balsam) on the higher slopes and summit—brought high praise. The cascading stream beside the way added its own charm and beauty.

When the party reached the top, the clouds were down over the mountain, and a little shower fell during the night. The whole group was disheartened. They feared that they were to be denied the thrilling views which the park leaders had expected and hoped for. When they set out for Myrtle Point early the next morning to see the sunrise—if any—only the highest peaks rose above the solid bank of clouds that filled the gorges below them. Fortunately, however, the clouds were soon dissipated, and the sun rose on a clear and beautiful day.

The things they saw as they slowly climbed the mountain were varied and interesting, but best of all were the breath-taking views from Myrtle Point and Cliff Top, the principal vantage points on the summit of Mt. Le Conte. As they stood on the former, they could see, far below them, the virgin hardwood forests of the Greenbrier wilderness area. All around them and on the distant heights were the fine virgin stands of red spruce and the pleasing contrast of many exposed ridges clad in the lower-growing rhododendron and myrtle. One of the most distant points was Mt. Guyot, on the Tennessee–North Carolina state line, second highest mountain in the Smokies. Nearer, and also on the state line, was the jagged crest appropriately known as "the Sawtooth Range," with the Jump-Off at the west end. From Cliff Top they looked down on towering Chimney Tops far below them and, beyond that precipitous twin-topped mountain, on fir-clad Clingmans Dome, highest point in the Smokies (6,643 feet).

Mt. Le Conte, their grandstand vantage point, is the third highest peak in the Smokies—falling only slightly below Guyot and Clingmans Dome in elevation above sea level. From that lofty position, however, the two park-hunting guests made an interesting discovery. When on Cliff Top, they had seen the edges of Gatlinburg nestling more than a vertical mile below them. But it was here on Le Conte that they learned firsthand that height above sea level is not necessarily the significant measure of a mountain's height, or "tallness"; instead, elevation from immediate base to summit is the impression that strikes the observer. The 5,301-feet difference between Gatlinburg's 1,292 and Le Conte's 6,593 feet makes Mt. Le Conte the tallest mountain—highest above its immediate base—in the eastern United States.

Advance preparations for this trip, made by Conservation Association officials, had included shelter for eighteen persons near the summit of Le Conte. So great was the interest in the trip, however, that there were twenty-five in the party. This meant that seven younger members of the group had a real experience of roughing it and *trying* to sleep in the open. Today, in contrast, Le Conte Lodge provides comfortable lodging and appetizing meals for as many as forty persons each night, except in winter. Even yet, however, the only way to reach the Lodge is by "shank's mare" or horseback.

Thus ended the trip up, by way of the north slope. After the night in the shelter or under the stars and time enough in the morning to feast their eyes on the gorgeous views, the party began the extremely steep descent by another route—the south slope, via Alum Cave Bluff. This "trail" lacked the boulders of the upward climb, but the heavily wooded mountainside was so steep that to stand erect without holding to a tree or shrub was a real feat. The climax came as they slowly worked their way around the huge overhanging cliff that is known as Alum Cave Bluff. Some climbed down a tree, the top of which reached just above the upper edge of the cliff, but others went farther around and virtually slid down the almost perpendicular slope.

Weather, which regularly smiled on those early trips for important visitors, was particularly good for this eventful trip to Mt. Le Conte. A hard rain a few hours before the start had washed the atmosphere of the characteristic haze—which, incidentally, contributed the "Smoky" part of this park's official name. The storm had given a pleasing freshness to the trees and shrubs and had added volume and interest to the crystal-clear streams.

Because of a considerably confused nomenclature, one phase of the well-laid plans for this trip went amiss. Leaders had arranged for horses to meet the party as far up as they could be taken— a spot then known to many as Grassy Patch, but known to some by the name of the man who had occupied a crude cabin there. But to the man who was to deliver the horses "Grassy Patch" meant *"the* grassy patch" at Indian Gap, about ten miles away; and that is where he sent the horses. This misunderstanding made it necessary for the already tired party to walk some seven extra miles. As can well be understood, it was a weary and footsore group that finally reached Gatlinburg. In fact, two or three of the men, including Mr. Davis, needed help long before reaching Grassy Patch— now Alum Cave Bluff parking area. Yes, very tired, but supremely happy!

27

The two Washington committeemen were taken to other parts of the Smokies, also. They were much pleased with the quiet charm of Cades Cove and its surrounding wall of mountains. This gave them some idea of the highly varied types of mountains that make up the Great Smokies. They were also fascinated by the grassy balds that overlook Cades Cove from their perch on the main crest. These mountaintop meadows—or "meadows in the sky," as they are sometimes called—are not above timberline, but the reason for the absence of trees is still a mystery to botanist-ecologists. On Gregory Bald they saw flame azaleas ringing the edge of the grass and running down in a wide border into the forests. In late June, when these azaleas are in bloom, Gregory Bald is a major show place of the Smokies. Although he did not see them in bloom on this particular trip, Mr. Kelsey, an internationally famous botanist and nurseryman, recognized the flame azalea as still another attraction of the area. He stated that it reaches its maximum development on and near Gregory Bald.

Other members of the committee came later and were similarly thrilled. With their field inspection trips finally completed, the group returned to Washington and began a long series of conferences, in which one after another of the less desirable sites was eliminated.

Loye W. Miller, then a reporter for the *Knoxville News,* was one of those younger fellows who had had to sleep in the open during that important night on Mt. Le Conte. Shortly after the close of the inspection trip, he quoted members of the committee as having said that no other site they had seen compared with the Great Smokies in grandeur and variety of interest. They found it impossible, however, to narrow the field to the *one* best area, all things considered; and it soon developed that accessibility was to play a large part in the final selection.

The big announcement came on December 13, 1924. The recommendation was for establishment of *two* new parks: the first was to be in the Blue Ridge Mountains of Virginia (Shenandoah National Park), its proximity to centers of population being cited; but the recommendation for a second, or later, park in the Great Smokies carried some very high and significant praise for this area.

28

HOAR FROST:
This is the way
forests on Mt. Le
Conte looked on
January 1, 1928,
when the delega-
tion of scientists
visited the moun-
tain in 20-below-
zero weather. The
striking "frozen
fog" forms when
clouds are down
on the mountains
in freezing tem-
perature. On the
wind-swept sum-
mits, the frost
forms "banners of
ice" which project
into the wind.

—Jim Thompson

DEEP CREEK WATERSHED (*above*): Some of the rugged land on the North Carolina side of the park can be seen in this view of Deep Creek watershed, photographed from near Newfound Gap.

CADES COVE (*below*): Over 3,000 acres of level land are surrounded by a wall of mountains in picturesque Cades Cove. This is the view that was shown to both delegations of Tennessee legislators and other important visitors in the early stages of the park movement.

Height of Mountains—Depth of Valleys

"The Great Smokies easily stand first because of the height of mountains, depth of valleys, ruggedness of the area, and the *unexampled variety* of trees, shrubs and plants," the committee said in its official report.[1] The statement went on:

This region includes Mt. Guyot, Mt. Le Conte, Clingmans Dome and Gregory Bald, and may be extended in several directions to include other splendid mountain regions adjacent thereto.

The Great Smokies have some handicaps which will make their development a matter of delay; their very ruggedness and height make road and other park development a serious undertaking as to time and expense. The Blue Ridge of Virginia . . . while secondary to the Great Smokies, in altitude and some other features, constitutes in our judgment the outstanding and logical place for the first national park in the Southern Appalachians. We hope it will be made into a national park and that its success will encourage Congress to create a second national park in the Great Smoky Mountains.

This announcement brought mixed reactions. To most of the park workers it was regarded as a great victory, as the first major accomplishment in the then-young movement. To Colonel Chapman, however, it was bitterly disappointing to see an admittedly "inferior" area recommended for first establishment as a national park. He accused members of the Southern Appalachian Committee of departing from their established standard or measure for a national park and implied that "pressure" from Washington had influenced the decision.

Edward J. Meeman, editor of the *Knoxville News,* immediately published a strong editorial in which he urged tolerance and asked that members of the committee not be criticized for selecting the Blue Ridge area to be developed first. "Let there be only a short interval, or No INTERVAL AT ALL, between the first and the second new national park," he pleaded.[2]

[1] According to Dr. A. J. Sharp, head of the Department of Botany of the University of Tennessee, the Great Smokies have 130 species of native trees as compared with less than 150 kinds in all Europe and less than 20 in some of our Western national parks.

[2] *Knoxville News,* December 16, 1924.

Many North Carolinians resented the selection of the Great Smokies, even though the Shenandoah site might very likely be established first. In the Waynesville and Bryson City areas, however, there was great rejoicing, as in Tennessee. Horace Kephart, famous author of *Our Southern Highlanders* and other books, had favored and worked for the Great Smokies project, as had Judge Thad Bryson. They were two of the very few prominent North Carolinians who opposed the Grandfather Mountain-Linville Gorge proposal and fought for the Great Smokies instead.

Other North Carolinians, especially those in the Asheville, Linville, Blowing Rock, and Boone communities, still clung to their first choice, however, and fought against the Great Smokies project. Several of them owned extensive tracts of virgin timber in the Smokies, whereas much of the other site had already been cut over. Their opposition to the Great Smokies persisted until members of Secretary Work's committee issued the following stern warning:

> Owing to the opposition of certain interests in North Carolina to the original plan for a national park in the Great Smoky Mountains, the Commission may find it necessary to modify its boundary as originally contemplated and consider the advisability of the creation of a national park which will be largely in the state of Tennessee.[3]

Following receipt of that ultimatum, a meeting was held by a large number of North Carolina's leading citizens at Asheville's Battery Park Hotel. It was recognized unmistakably that they had lost their fight for the Grandfather Mountain-Linville Gorge location.[4] They also realized that a park in the Great Smokies was the next best choice. Upon the motion of Plato D. Ebbs the group voted to give undivided support to the Great Smokies movement. This they did to the fullest extent.

---

[3] *Knoxville Journal,* July 21, 1925.

[4] Much of the fine Linville Gorge area has since been made a part of the Blue Ridge Parkway and is thus being preserved for the enjoyment of the whole public. Although, as mentioned above, most of the virgin timber had already been removed from the slopes of Grandfather Mountain prior to 1924, thrilling views of the surrounding country are afforded from the rugged summit, which is reached by a toll road.

UNMATCHED VARIETY: In a fifteen-mile trip in the Great Smokies one can see as many trees—many of them giants of their species—as are found in a trip from the Smokies to Canada. This half-million-acre park exhibits almost as many kinds of native trees (130 species) as does all of Europe.

RAMSEY CASCADES: Deep in the Greenbrier wilderness section of the Great Smokies is the beautiful waterfall at left. It is the destination of many hikes.

MT. CAMMERER: This 5,025-foot peak, at the northeast end of the Smokies, was named as a tribute and memorial to Arno B. Cammerer, former director of the National Park Service.

—Jim Thompson

CHAPTER 4

FIRST LARGE TRACT PURCHASED

WHILE CHOICE of a park site was being decided, there was considerable activity in Knoxville looking toward the purchase of the first large tract for the proposed park. At the very outset, in 1924, the selection of this site was closely tied in with the campaign for governor by Austin Peay, who was seeking the Democratic nomination, usually tantamount to election in Tennessee. Colonel Claude S. Reeder and other friends convinced Peay that it would be politically wise for him to espouse the cause of the proposed Great Smoky Mountains National Park and that he should have the state buy the tract of the Little River Lumber Company, on the Tennessee side of the park. So thoroughly favorable was Peay to the park idea and the suitability of this tract that he pledged to make a state park of it if a national park should not materialize. He even got an option on the land from Colonel W. B. Townsend, principal owner, giving the state until February 1, 1925, to make the purchase at a per-acre price which brought the total to $273,557 for the 76,507 acres. Timber had already been cut from most of the property, and the company was still cutting; and, in fact, the option and later purchase contract provided that the company might continue cutting for another fifteen years.

Mr. Peay won the nomination and election. Mrs. W. P. Davis, "mother" of the park idea and at that time a member of the Lower House of the Tennessee legislature, was given the privilege of introducing the bill providing for the purchase of the Little River tract. This was done early in the 1925 session. Despite the fact that Governor Peay was actively supporting the bill—and to the surprise of Mr. Davis, Colonel Chapman, and other park workers—

strong opposition was met, and there was grave concern about the passage of the bill.

To stimulate interest among the lawmakers, the Knoxville Chamber of Commerce raised a special fund of $5,000 to charter a special train to bring to Knoxville the entire legislature and state officials—including many minor officials, secretaries, and the like. Although there were only 132 members of the legislature (99 house members and 33 senators), there were approximately 200 persons on that special train.

From Knoxville they were taken in private automobiles over the old Rich Mountain road to the point where, as they picnicked, they could get a sweeping view of picturesque Cades Cove and the rampart of mountains beyond. They were then driven back to Townsend, at the edge of the park, to board the train again for a ride up spectacular Little River Gorge. It had been some time since the timber was cut from this route, and the second growth was getting a good start at reforestation. At Elkmont they were entertained and given further information about the proposed park and about the pending bill for the purchase of the big tract through which they had been traveling. It was another instance of perfect weather for an important trip.

Park leaders felt confident that the bill would pass, perhaps easily, after the visit of the legislators. They had, however, underestimated the bitterness of the opposition that was to be led by James B. Wright, an attorney for the Louisville & Nashville Railroad; and most certainly they had underestimated Mr. Wright's power and influence with members of the legislature, among whom he had a wide acquaintance. From the very beginning—at the meeting in Judge Lindsay's office on December 21, 1923—Wright had favored and worked for a national forest in the Great Smokies and had fought the idea of a national park at every step of the way. In all fairness it should here be remembered that at the first two meetings in 1923 the whole group, with the exception of Mr. Davis, had entertained the idea of a national forest *or* a national park. The main difference between Wright's attitude and the others' is that he stuck tenaciously to the campaign for a national forest.

So successful was the campaign of the Wright forces that the bill failed in the Lower House on April 8, 1925, after having passed the

Senate by a 20 to 12 vote a week earlier. It was a dejected delegation of park supporters who watched that stinging defeat.

A less determined group would have given up, and the park movement would doubtless have died at that point. But not so Mr. Davis. Not so the tenacious fighter, Colonel Chapman. And not so Ben A. Morton, a staunch leader in the movement. A series of conferences led to the introduction of a new bill, differing from the other in one important respect. It provided that the city of Knoxville—the city government, not the citizens independently—should pay one-third of the purchase price. It also provided that the state was not to be obligated unless or until the federal government had agreed to accept the land and use it as a part of the park.

Many people believed that the city had no legal right to spend tax money for a non-city project, especially when that project was not even in Knox County, in which Knoxville is located. This view was held, secretly, even by some of the park leaders. More important, however, was the fact that it was held by some of the men who had been fighting the park movement, especially this particular Little River project. These men were so firmly convinced that the city could not legally participate in the purchase that they voted for the bill in full confidence that the city council would kill it for them. But this aid gave the affirmative vote a comfortable majority; and on April 10, 1925, Governor Peay signed the bill into law, using a special quill pen, which was then given to Mrs. Davis. This became the second in a large number of major accomplishments, without any one of which the movement might well have failed.

On the day following the signing of the Little River bill, the Conservation Association passed a resolution asking Governor Peay to appoint Colonel Chapman as the East Tennessee member of the Tennessee State Park and Forestry Commission, the then-dormant body that had been given the task of handling details of the Little River purchase. It also voted to add the word "Great" to the Association's name, thus recognizing *Great* Smoky Mountains as the official and full name of the mountains in which the park was to be located. It should be recalled that at first the group unofficially designated itself the "Smoky Mountain Forest Reserve Association."

In compliance with the request of the Conservation Association,

33

on August 7, 1925, Governor Peay named Colonel Chapman, Henry Colton, of Nashville, and A. E. Markham, of Tiptonville, as members of the commission. Colonel Chapman was made chairman, in recognition of the fact that he was already becoming the unquestioned leader of the movement.

It is obvious that a tremendous amount of work had already been done. But the movement was still in its infancy, as later became apparent. No one seemed to know just what lay ahead, and developments came at a veritable snail's pace until, on March 11, 1926, Ben A. Morton, then mayor of Knoxville under its new city-manager form of government, and a most effective park worker, called a meeting "to save the movement." The result was that on March 30 the city council voted to pay the requested one-third of the purchase price for the Little River Lumber Company tract. That was not an easy thing to do, but it was not the fear of legal obstacles that caused the most concern among park leaders.

To bring the situation into proper focus it is necessary to take a look at Knoxville politics of that time. Under the newly adopted city-manager government, the city had been able to get a council of eleven men who were outstanding business and civic leaders. One of these has already been mentioned—Ben A. Morton, a top-ranking man in business and financial circles, in church activities, and in public and civic matters. He had never engaged in political campaigns except to cast his ballot. He and the other businessmen on the new non-political council had been virtually drafted for this public service by an aroused electorate. Morton was then chosen unanimously by his fellow councilmen to serve as mayor, with industrialist and civic leader Weston M. Fulton as vice-mayor. Never before had Knoxville had the services of such distinguished men.

All went well for several months. It was not long, however, until this unusually strong council and the equally strong city manager were subjected to a campaign of interference from political-minded persons, most of whom had fought the city-manager plan from the beginning. Members of the council were annoyed by telephone calls at all hours of the night. Among other things, the council was accused of municipal extravagance. There were rumors of a recall, and these soon developed into reality. Four of the eleven members were confronted with a recall election in which three of them were defeated by men who had pledged "strict economy."[1] At least two of the pre-recall members were known to be "economy" minded, especially after they saw the fate of their colleagues. Park leaders wondered if there were possibly others.

It was the first meeting of the changed council to which was presented the resolution to pay one-third of the cost of the Little River Lumber Company tract, in Sevier and Blount counties. New members of the council made it clear that they did not want Colonel Chapman to address the meeting in behalf of the resolution. Therefore, rather than risk a vote on that point, Mayor Morton posed numerous questions, all of which called for answers from Colonel Chapman, with the result that the dynamic park leader used up a large part of the time in answering the specific questions. Mayor Morton read a telegram from Governor Peay announcing that the state was ready to proceed when and if the city of Knoxville should decide officially to pay one-third of the purchase price. Some of the councilmen sought to delay action for a period of six months but were not able to get enough votes to make the postponement. When the question was finally put to a vote, the results were six for participating with the state and five against it. Seeing that they had lost their efforts to block the purchase, all five opponents changed their votes, and the official result was unanimous for the city's participation.

A showdown on the legality of city bonds issued for that specific purpose was later avoided when Colonel Townsend, principal owner of the Little River Lumber Company, announced that his company would accept the bonds at par.

The company's tract of 76,507 acres bought at a price of $273,557 shows an average cost of only $3.57 per acre.

Possible Because It Was Impossible

Purchase of the Little River tract was one of the all-important steps that were actually made possible because so many people believed them to be impossible. If several members of the Tennessee legislature had had the least idea that the Knoxville City Council could or would pay one-third of the purchase price for this tract,

[1] *Knoxville Sentinel,* March 1, 1926.

it is reasonably certain that the bill would have been killed in the legislature, as was the original bill which called for the state to pay the entire purchase price.

This was the third major accomplishment in the unique park movement.

Boundary Lines Set

Along with the many other activities in the latter part of 1924 and 1925, leaders in both states were making detailed studies of possible boundary lines for the park. There were those who wanted to confine it to the higher elevations, thus leaving out the mountain farms lower down the slopes. Arno B. Cammerer, then associate director of the National Park Service, was assigned the task of determining the boundary within which the park would be established. While working in Swain County, North Carolina, he was ably assisted by Horace Kephart and Dr. Kelly Bennett, of Bryson City. Harlan P. Kelsey, a former North Carolinian, already introduced as a member of the Southern Appalachian Committee, was also an advisor; and Verne Rhoades, of Asheville, prompted a decision that made the final border in Haywood County, North Carolina, include all of the Cataloochee watershed rather than follow Cataloochee Creek.

It was General Frank Maloney, of Knoxville, however, who worked most closely with Cammerer on the entire border—as to both purchase area and actual park border. He had a double qualification for this work. First of all, he had been making extensive hiking and camping trips throughout the Smokies since 1896. Secondly, as a civil engineer with long and varied experience, he could see and understand more about the character and topography of mountain lands by studying topographic maps than most men could on the ground.

The purchase area of 704,000 acres was fixed in 1925 and was shown on a special new map in 1926. This map, widely used at the time, was known as the "Cammerer map" or the "red line map."

CHAPTER 5

WANTED: MONEY AND PUBLICITY

IN THE MEANTIME intensive fund-raising campaigns were being waged in both park states. Initial efforts in this respect, undertaken in Knoxville, had met with discouraging results. The first goal was for only $50,000, with which to finance the already heavy travel expense and promotion activities. When it became obvious that this modest sum was not to be raised on a strictly local level, it was decided that the much larger goal—for purchase and promotion—could not be considered without the help of professional fund-raisers.

In October of 1925 the Conservation Association and its North Carolina counterpart, Great Smoky Mountains, Inc., signed a contract with a nationally known firm of fund-raisers. After weeks of systematic preparations, during which a considerable amount of enthusiasm was developed, a campaign was launched on December 7, 1925, with a goal of $415,000, by an "army" of 250 workers. Almost $100,000 was reported in the Knoxville campaign during the first two days, in which the host of workers called upon individuals and firms which had been assigned to them. The workers and the speakers at campaign rallies stressed the point that the money subscribed was in reality an investment, not a gift. Senator Mark Squires of North Carolina called attention to the fact that, in addition to being a good investment, this park would be even more important as the means of saving virgin forests for the education and inspiration of future generations.

Colonel Chapman set the pace with a personal subscription of $5,000, in addition to pledges by businesses in which he was interested. Some of the corporations pledged as much as $10,000. "National Park Founders' Certificates" were given to all subscribers, in which it was stated that each donor was "entitled to the particular respect and gratitude of visitors who throughout the years and ages will benefit by the vision and generosity of those who have made possible the preservation of the virgin forests and varied flora of the choicest section of the Southern Appalachian Mountains." The Founders' Certificates were signed in the name of the Interstate National Park Committee by D. C. Chapman, chairman, and P. D. Ebbs, of Asheville, secretary.

It was, however, to be no whirlwind campaign, but a long-drawn-out affair. By the middle of February the reported pledges in Tennessee amounted to only $268,825, most of which came from Knoxville. With the drive lagging again, Mr. Morton issued a call for one hundred new workers. Colonel Chapman, Mr. Davis, and scores of other workers urged support of the park movement. Mr. Kelsey, one of the committee of five who had selected the Great Smokies, made a rousing plea for greater speed in fund-raising. The Community Chest postponed its annual drive so as not to interfere with the park fund drive. Motorcades carried the plea to practically every city and village in the eastern part of the state.

An important phase of the campaign, perhaps even more so psychologically than financially, was the $1,391.72 given by more than 4,500 school children in Knox, Blount, Cocke and Sevier counties of Tennessee. These subscriptions were made in response to impassioned appeals for their help in establishing the park. The emphasis was to get as many contributors as possible, regardless of how small the amounts. Many of the children gave only a penny or two. A majority gave either a nickel, a dime or a quarter. A fair number gave either fifty cents or one dollar—very few more than a dollar. The average school-child contribution was thirty-one cents.

A new enthusiasm had been created, influenced considerably by the large number of gifts from children, and the Tennessee goal was reached and was increased to $600,000. On April 2, 1926, Colonel Chapman happily announced that the enlarged goal had not merely been reached, but actually oversubscribed—the reported gifts and pledges then standing at $604,000!

J. L. (Bud) Deaver, wholesale drygoods merchant, was given a silver loving cup which was inscribed to show that he was captain of the team which turned in the largest amount of subscriptions. Even though later information revealed that the announced total included the amount voted by the Knoxville City Council and that audits revealed a considerable number of duplications in reported pledges, this drive was recognized as Knoxville's outstanding and most successful money raising campaign.

North Carolina's campaign was launched December 1, 1925, with Colonel Chapman as the principal speaker for the kick-off meeting. The sponsoring group was the newly organized Great Smoky Mountains, Inc., the organization corresponding to Tennessee's Conservation Association and under the same professional guidance. This drive progressed much the same as that on the Tennessee side. It is possible, however, that the Carolina appeal was made a bit easier because residents of that state had been tourist-conscious for a relatively long time. It is also possible that the 1899–1901 effort to get a national park and the related and successful later effort to get national forests may have caused people on the eastern side of the mountains to be more readily receptive—once they had abandoned their zeal for locating the national park in their preferred Grandfather Mountain-Linville Gorge area.

At the time that the Tennessee workers announced the success of their campaign the North Carolina gifts and pledges had reached a total of approximately $400,000 with more coming in daily. On April 23 the Asheville Chamber of Commerce voted to underwrite the final $35,000 so as to meet the North Carolina goal of $500,000.

The successful fund-raising campaigns constituted the fourth major accomplishment of the park movement.

Throughout the early part of the movement, up to and through the various efforts to get the necessary money for land purchases, park leaders took full advantage of any and every legitimate possibility of favorable publicity for the Great Smokies. The rare beauty and rugged splendor of the area was told in word and picture at every opportunity.

Some "good ideas" were unsuccessful, of course, or were slow to mature—as, for example, the attempt to interest the *National Geo-*

39

graphic Magazine in publishing a story on the area and the park movement at this time. Features appeared, nevertheless, in some smaller magazines and in many newspapers. Beautiful pictures were sent out in large numbers, some by the Conservation Association, some by the Chamber of Commerce, some by the Automobile Club, and some by interested individuals. This was one point at which there was widespread cooperation.

In July of 1925, when writers and photographers from far and wide were covering the famous Scopes "monkey trial" at nearby Dayton, Tennessee, park leaders went to Dayton to invite both the principals and the writers to visit the proposed national park. Perhaps merely for the pleasant change from duties or perhaps partly also because of interest in the mountains, practically all accepted. As a matter of tact, it was decided to invite the principals for separate occasions—Clarence Darrow, John Scopes, and other defense personnel to make the visit on one weekend and William Jennings Bryan, chief prosecution attorney, at another time.

First to come was the large group of writers, most of whom represented newspapers in the nation's larger cities and two of whom represented London papers. Each local park enthusiast was assigned not more than two guests so that all visitors would be sure to get the important news about the projected park.

The party drove to beautiful and picturesque Cades Cove, stopping at strategic points to enjoy the thrilling panoramic views, at first looking down into the Cove from the road high above it and later from the floor of the Cove, looking up to the state line or main crest of the Smokies, from Thunderhead to Gregory Bald. After being driven as far through the Cove as the cars could go, the visitors were taken for a brief walk along a sparkling mountain stream into the edge of the virgin forest. One writer, whose wife was with him, delivered an interesting bit of conservation or anti-vandalism philosophy as he reprimanded her for picking a flower. "You shouldn't have done that," he said. "As long as it was growing beside the trail, it belonged to you and to everybody else. Now that you've picked it, it will soon die and won't belong to anyone."

Many interesting stories about the plans for the new national park were published as a result of this visit.

On the following weekend Mr. Darrow, Mr. Scopes, and a few

WANTED: MONEY AND PUBLICITY

others were taken on a somewhat longer trip to a point where the trail "topped out" on a high ridgecrest which afforded inspiring views. Mr. Darrow indicated great enthusiasm for the proposed national park.

Bryan's Last Act?

When Mr. and Mrs. Bryan were invited, Bryan indicated a willingness to see the Great Smokies, but expressed even greater interest in making two religious talks in Knoxville while enroute to the mountains. His wife protested that what he needed most was a good rest. Seizing upon Mrs. Bryan's concern as a means of clinching the acceptance, the delegation quickly offered the use of a mountain cottage, with privacy, where Bryan could rest and enjoy refreshing scenery and the invigorating atmosphere. He accepted that offer, but could not then fix the date. It was agreed that, as soon as he knew just when he would make the trip from Dayton to the Smokies, he should notify the writer.

On mid-afternoon of Sunday, July 26, Bryan did call to say that he and Mrs. Bryan would come on the following Tuesday, agreeing to be met at the Knoxville city limits and escorted to the cabin near Elkmont. It was less than an hour later when a newspaper friend called to report that William Jennings Bryan had died during his afternoon nap. It is likely, therefore, that, as was stated in newspaper dispatches announcing his death, his final act prior to that fateful nap was to complete his plans for the intended visit and rest in the Great Smokies.

Friendly Rivals

Another activity, arranged and carried out in early February of 1926 by the Knoxville Chamber of Commerce and designed specifically to create sentiment for the national park, was a nine-day trip throughout Florida by almost two hundred Knoxville and East Tennessee citizens, traveling by special train. Included in the group were all sixty-three members of the Knoxville High School Band. To be sure that this excellent band would make the best possible impression as they marched through the streets of various cities of the Sunshine State—east coast, interior and west coast—a steam suit-pressing machine was set up in a baggage car so that their uniforms could be freshly pressed every night.

Banquets were given for the group at the cities where overnight stops were made. Park leaders had opportunities to tell about the glories of the Great Smokies, which they did in eloquent style. Floridians, of course, also used this "captive audience" to sing the praises of their own state. During train stops for side trips, the motorcades nearly always managed somehow to pass through very attractive new subdivisions. On such occasions it was interesting to hear the two groups trying to outtalk each other. But all was in good spirit, for it was agreed that they were not competitors, since Florida —at that time—catered largely to winter visitors and the Great Smokies would be chiefly a summer attraction.

Twenty Below Zero

Another publicity effort, which included a second attempt to interest the *National Geographic,* had just succeeded when other developments made temporary postponement of activity in this direction seem wise. This began with a visit by fifty scientists, at the end of the mid-winter meeting of the American Association for the Advancement of Science (AAAS) at Nashville. They arrived in Knoxville in the early morning of the last day of 1927, ready to start for an eventful climb of Mt. Le Conte as guests of the Knoxville Chamber of Commerce. It was a mild winter morning, about 40° above zero, as they were met by the twenty-five Knoxvillians who were to be their hosts for the mountain trip. Starting from Cherokee Orchard, the hikers noticed that the temperature had dropped and snow was falling. By the time they reached the summit of grand old Mt. Le Conte, it was zero and the snow had stopped. That was before the days of the comfortable Le Conte Lodge, and members of the party were to have slept on balsam-bough beds in a tightly chinked, dirt-floored log cabin. But it was so cold that the blaze in the big fireplace made very little impression, and there was no sleeping that night. The time was spent in singing, telling stories and writing limericks about all of those present. A bucket of water sitting within ten feet of the fireplace froze solid.

Early the next morning, when most of the group trudged over the frozen snow to see the sunrise from Myrtle Point, almost a mile from the cabin, the thermometer registered 20° *below zero*—a drop of sixty degrees in less than twenty-four hours! This was not a

42

purely local situation, however, as was learned later: it was a nation-wide blizzard that had hit on that first day of 1928.

No such freakish weather had been anticipated, and some of the visiting scientists, especially those from warmer parts of the country, were much too lightly clad for such an experience. For example, a woman botanist from a Midwestern college was wearing silk hose and oxfords instead of the boots and woolen socks usually worn on mountain trips.

The late Dr. George E. Nichols, a botanist from Yale, expressed the sentiments of many others as they virtually crawled over ice-coated boulders in the vicinity of Rainbow Falls. "This will be a wonderful memory," Dr. Nichols said, "but I'll be darned glad when it *is* a memory."

One of the main reasons for inviting the scientists to make this trip had been the hope that they might help to get a story in the *National Geographic Magazine*. At least half of them wrote to the magazine within a short time after the trip, asking that a staff member be sent to write up the Smokies and the proposed national park. Soon afterward the *Geographic* editor agreed to comply.

But in this short interim momentous developments—to be explained in Chapter 9—made this long-sought publicity undesirable for the time being. It was doubtless a surprised *Geographic* staff that received and granted the request of park leaders to postpone the publication of a Great Smokies story.

CHAPTER 6

VICTORY CREATES
OVERCONFIDENCE

WHILE money and publicity were being sought, plans also went forward in Congress for enacting legislation to authorize the park. The original plan of Secretary Work's committee had been to create Shenandoah National Park first. The later proposal of the National Park Service for simultaneous establishing of the Smokies met with immediate Virginian protest, which did not subside until Secretary Work issued a stern warning to the effect that it was both or neither so far as his approval was concerned.

The bill, as introduced in the Senate by Senator Claude A. Swanson of Virginia, provided that the Great Smoky Mountains National Park could be taken over for administration when at least 300,000 contiguous acres had been turned over by the two states and accepted by the Secretary of the Interior, and that it could be considered as established and ready for development as soon as a major portion of the 704,000 acres had been deeded and accepted. Colonel Chapman, insisting that the 300,000 minimum was too high, succeeded in getting the bill amended so as to permit acceptance for protection and administration as soon as 150,000 acres had been turned over officially. The amended bill was then introduced in the House by Congressman Temple of Pennsylvania, on April 14, and was passed on May 15 without a dissenting vote—the only way in which it could have been brought up so near adjournment time. It was signed into law by President Calvin Coolidge on May 22, 1926.

Before actual passage, the bill was made to include also Mammoth Cave National Park, in Kentucky. This park, although meritorious, was not expected to be authorized at that time, but such was the

Brownlow School.

Oakwood School

Central High School

Name	Pledge	Cash	1927
Roy Underwood			
Herbert Vesser	05	05	
A. Kenneth Vise	50	50	
Ruth Vise	1 00	1 00	
Mossie Walker	10	10	
William Walker	05	05	
Mrs. Gladys Wallace	50	50	
Marie Wallace	25	25	
Ruby E. Walsh	05	05	
Charlie Warters	15	25	
J. D. Warters	25	25	
James Warwick	10	10	
Blanche Waters	05	05	
James Waters	05	05	
Thelma Waters	10	10	
Ralph Watson	10	10	
Willie Mae Watts	25	25	
Mary Lynn Weaver	05	05	
Lucia Webb	05	05	
Ruth Webb	10	10	
Herbert M. Webster	10	10	
Anna A. Weigel	10	10	
Helma Lee White	1 00	1 00	
Nelle White	05	05	
Margaret Wight	05	05	
Mary Lee Wight	10	10	
Ned Wiley, Jr.	15	15	
Francis Wilkerson	25	25	
Ethel Williams	25	25	
Jessie L. Williams	05	05	
Beulah Willis	25	25	
Jennie Wilson	05	05	
Margaret Wilson	05	05	
Blanche Wininger	05	05	
Pauline Halback	05	05	
Cana Hood	10	10	
Reba Hood	25	25	
June B. Woolrich	10	10	
Grace Wright	1 00	1 00	
Madeline Young	05	05	

Maryville School

SCHOOL CHILDREN HELPED: Bringing in their pennies, dimes, and dollars, school children supported the park movement with enthusiasm.

CHIMNEY TOPS: An enlargement of this picture was taken to Asheville in 1924 by the Conservation Association delegation when it enlisted the interest of two members of Secretary Work's committee. The twin-topped peak is a symbol of the Great Smokies. Chimneys Campground now occupies the area in the right foreground.

—*Jim Thompson*

outcome as the lucky result of a Congressional tradition or regulation. It was the practice, near the close of any session of Congress, to permit the introduction of only such bills as could get "unanimous consent." Mammoth Cave advocates refused to give "unanimous consent" to the Shenandoah and Great Smokies authorization bill unless the Kentucky park should also be included. Thus, three parks rather than the intended two were authorized.

Passage of the bill by Congress authorizing the establishment of a park in the Great Smokies brought major accomplishment number five.

News that the bill had passed was received with great joy by the hundreds of dedicated park workers in Tennessee and North Carolina. The rejoicing was accompanied, however, by timely warnings that park enthusiasts should "keep their heads." The *Knoxville Sentinel* published a strong editorial in which it referred to the Great Smokies as "Sacred Ground," and not a place for profit-taking.

The Knoxville Automobile Club staged a huge "victory banquet" for Colonel Chapman at Whittle Springs Hotel on the night of Friday, May 28, on his return from Washington, where he had observed the passage of the bill. The Colonel was presented a large silver loving cup as a token of the high esteem in which he was held and in appreciation of the excellent work he had done. There was general elation. Dancing, singing, and an exhibit of natural-color pictures of the Smokies were other scheduled features of the banquet.

The expressions of appreciation to Chapman and to his numerous co-workers were proper and good. But the feeling that the victory had actually been won was to be short-lived. New and increasingly difficult problems were to be faced in rapid succession before a final victory could be enjoyed. Actually, the very feeling that the fight had been won merely contributed to some of the forthcoming problems and heartaches. There was a definite letdown in activities. Colonel Chapman, in an effort to get some needed rest, took a long-delayed trip to Europe, leaving in mid-summer and not returning until October. During his absence other leaders in the movement, accustomed to following his lead and backing up his efforts, also rested, at least insofar as major park activities were concerned.

The opposition took no vacation, however. James B. Wright, who had fought the park from the beginning and still insisted on a national forest, held a big meeting at Elkmont on Labor Day, 1926. It was attended by highway officials of both Tennessee and North Carolina, by a North Carolina hotel man who was "noted for his activity in promoting seven national highways," by the North Carolina owner of a large acreage just across the state line from the Little River tract, and by residents "from every cove in the Smokies."[1] The announced purpose of the meeting was to promote road building. It was proposed that good roads should connect every cove with every other cove. Mr. Wright told of having converted the old railroad bed from Elkmont up Little River to Fishcamp to a usable automobile road. He announced the intention of extending that road to the state line in the vicinity of Silers Bald and connecting it with North Carolina roads then being planned to follow old logging railroad beds from Proctor up to the state line.[2]

One of the speakers at Mr. Wright's Elkmont meeting told of having built a road into relatively worthless property and thereby increasing its value to $1,000 per acre. The implication, of course, was that the large number of mountain men at the meeting could increase the value of their own land by helping to get roads built.

The most disheartening news was Colonel Townsend's announcement at the close of the meeting that there was no longer any option on his Little River Lumber Company tract; that the option—once extended orally—had expired before there was any acceptance.

"What has become of the park?" Townsend asked. "Where are the leaders of the park movement? Why aren't they doing something? I am vitally interested, and I want to know," he added.

It had been assumed that the oral extension was still in effect. This announcement came as a bombshell. The *Knoxville News* story, published the day after Mr. Wright's meeting, expressed fear that the repudiation of the Little River option and the extensive plans for road building in the mountains would lead to higher prices for land and might cause the death of the park movement.

On the next day, September 8, the *News* carried a strong editorial in which it severely criticized park leaders for the recent period of

[1] *Knoxville News*, September 7, 1926.
[2] *Ibid.*

46

inactivity. It praised Colonel Chapman for his "miraculous feat" in getting the park bill passed, but warned that the movement could not wait for the Colonel's return from Europe. The editorial further charged that a big and serious mistake had been not to get options on various large tracts, specifically the Ritter Lumber Company, in North Carolina. It stated that, when an effort was finally made to buy the Ritter tract, the land had already been sold to a real estate developer—one who attended the Wright meeting on Labor Day. It did, however, quote Chapman as having stated months earlier that the Southern Appalachian Park Commission had opposed the taking of options on land that was priced too high.

The *News* editorial stated that Mr. Wright had for a long time been wooing engineers and other officials of state highway departments, but apparently without success. It urged that Governor Peay not permit any road building until after the adjoining lands had been bought.

Maloney Suggests Solution

Following the publication of that rousing editorial, General Maloney went to Nashville for a conference with Governor Peay, in which Maloney urged that the Governor notify Colonel Townsend of the state's readiness to complete the purchase. He reminded the Governor that the legislative act of the previous year authorized him to buy the land when certain conditions had been met, especially when Congress should agree to use the land for a national park. He showed the Governor a copy of the bill which Congress had passed in May and also a copy of the *News* editorial.

Shortly before General Maloney's death he told the writer that Governor Peay then asked, "What can we do?"

"You should write to Colonel Townsend telling him that the state is ready to buy, and that you have instructed the attorney general to prepare title," Maloney replied.

Peay then dictated such a letter to Townsend, signed it and gave Maloney a copy. On his return to Knoxville Maloney called Townsend, who said that he had not received the Governor's letter and repeated the earlier statement that the option had expired. The next day, however, Townsend called Maloney and expressed a willingness to sell. On September 22 the directors of the Little River Lumber

Company authorized the sale. On November 13 Townsend, in a Nashville conference with the Governor, Maloney for the Conservation Association, and Ben A. Morton for the city of Knoxville, officially announced the willingness to sell at the original option price of $273,557.97 for the 76,507-acre tract. A *News* editorial on the following day complimented and thanked Colonel Townsend for not raising the price above that of the original option figure, stating that to have done so at that point could have been, and likely would have been, fatal to the whole park movement—especially coming before full momentum had been gained.

Preparation of the title and its examination by the Attorney General's office required several weeks. In this a total of 331 deeds of the Little River Company had to be checked and combined into one instrument—which, incidentally, contained 151 pages.

In the meantime, there had been an effort by park foes to get the 1927 legislature to pass a bill blocking or rescinding the Little River purchase. This bill received very little support—in fact, met with strong opposition. Even so, the *Nashville Banner* devoted column after column of antagonistic news stories in a fight on the purchase. By adding interest, loss of taxes, cost of protecting and policing for 20 years, it sought in one instance to show that the land was to cost the state over $2,000,000! This was not buried in fine print, but was displayed conspicuously in tabular form.[3] Park leaders argued, on the other hand, that this purchase was a bargain since the price was slightly over $3 per acre, whereas North Carolina had been paying from $9 to $12 per acre for similar land. On March 22 the deed was sent to Governor Peay, and the state's check for $182,371.73, its share of the cost, was given to Colonel Townsend.

This was the first large tract of land bought for the national park in either state. It also represented the sixth major accomplishment in the movement, and appeared to be the end of the long-drawn-out Little River fight.

"Conservation-with-an-Axe" Association

There was still a "fly in the ointment," however. There was considerable dissatisfaction with the provision of the purchase con-

[3] *Nashville Banner,* November 28, 1926.

tract, which allowed the company to continue cutting virgin timber for another fifteen years. Secretary Work indicated that the portion of the land on which cutting was still permitted could not be accepted for park purposes.

An extensive editorial campaign was waged by Edward J. Meeman, editor of the *Knoxville News* (which shortly became the *Knoxville News-Sentinel*). He called attention to the fact that one of the main reasons for establishing a national park, rather than a national forest, was to preserve for future generations the primitive beauty of the virgin forests. Day after day he hammered away in an effort to prevent the timber-cutting. In his long fight he sarcastically referred to the Great Smoky Mountains Conservation Association, the group which started the park movement and worked up the Little River purchase, as the "Conservation-with-an-Axe" Association.

This pointed criticism, coming from a man who had effectively supported various steps of the park movement, was a bitter pill for the park leaders. They knew that Mr. Meeman was exactly right in principle. They also knew, nevertheless, that there was no money then available and none in sight for the purchase of the remaining standing timber—which, incidentally, would have cost much more than the price paid for the land. They pointed out these facts to Mr. Meeman and expressed the belief that this purchase, even on the contract basis, would be a start from which further progress could be made, more money obtained, and other tracts of virgin timber saved. But, they indicated further, if this sale had not been made because of the lack of funds with which to stop timber-cutting immediately, the whole park movement would probably have died.

It took considerable time to convince Mr. Meeman that these were the cold, hard facts of the case. But he was finally convinced, announcing his belated approval in a big front-page editorial. In this editorial he explained that he still regretted to see the cutting, but that it was apparently the only way in which the park movement could be kept alive for the greater benefits that were to come. From that time on, the movement had no more loyal and effective supporter than Mr. Meeman and the *News-Sentinel*, which he edited.

CHAPTER 7

MEETING THE
NORTH CAROLINA CHALLENGE

HAVING once committed themselves to the Great Smokies and reluctantly given up the Grandfather Mountain-Linville Gorge dream, North Carolina park leaders put on a real burst of speed and for a time showed more progress than had been made recently in Tennessee. Under the spirited leadership of State Senator Mark Squires of Lenoir, a bill was presented to the 1927 session of the North Carolina legislature providing for the appropriation of $2,000,000 for the purchase of park lands in that state. The bill, more or less naturally, contained two qualifying safeguards concerning the North Carolina money: that it would not be made available until Tennessee provided a like amount and until enough appeared to be in hand, from all sources, to assure the completion of the park.

Although there was a considerable amount of support already created for the park bill, its passage was in doubt for a short time because of friction that had developed between Senator Squires and Governor Angus K. McLean. The park leader, somewhat nervous because of ill health, openly criticized the Governor in January, 1927, and it was feared that his attitude might cause the defeat of the bill. The situation was cleared, however, and the bill's passage assured as a result of the pacifying efforts of Dr. E. C. Brooks, president of North Carolina State College. He persuaded the Governor to support the bill despite the criticism he had received from Senator Squires.[1]

[1] *North Carolina Historical Review*, April, 1960, p. 174.

On February 12 the North Carolina Senate passed the bill by a vote of 14 to 7. On February 22 the House passed it by the overwhelming vote of 99 to 10. Thus was this seventh major accomplishment another instance in which the success was achieved because there were those who believed it to be impossible. Senator Squires told the writer that some senators had merely tried to "pass the buck" to Tennessee and that enough of them to have changed the results had admitted to him that they voted approval only because they believed that Tennessee could not and would not match their appropriation.

The bill provided for a North Carolina Park Commission of eleven members to handle land buying. Senator Squires was made chairman. The other members were Dr. Brooks, of Raleigh; Plato D. Ebbs, of Asheville, treasurer; Dave M. Buck, of Bald Mountain; John G. Dawson, of Kinston; Frank A. Linney, of Boone, succeeded in 1928 by Stuart W. Cramer, Jr., of Cramerton; E. S. Parker, Jr., of Greensboro; R. T. Fountain, of Rocky Mount; Harry L. Nettles, of Asheville; James A. Hardison, of Wadesboro; and J. Elmer Long, of Durham. Verne Rhoades, with the background of a professional forester, was made executive secretary. He handled the land acquisition program, including the surveys, land appraisals and multitudinous other details.

Governor McLean was a vigorous supporter of the appropriation bill, as were J. Elmer Long, president of the North Carolina Senate, and R. T. Fountain, speaker of the House. Other members of the newly appointed Commission who were also legislators and outspoken supporters of the park bill included Senator Squires, Messrs. Buck, Ebbs, Dawson and Nettles, and Congressman Zebulon Weaver (D., N. C.).

Charles A. Webb, owner-publisher of the *Asheville Citizen* and *Times,* was one of the most aggressive and most effective backers of the Great Smokies appropriation. The aid given by his papers was a big factor in the outcome of this appropriation that saved the park. Some years later his services were recognized by his appointment to fill a vacancy on the Park Commission.

Passage of the North Carolina bill served as a forceful challenge to Tennessee. Without that $2,000,000 appropriation it most likely would have been impossible to get another park appropriation passed by the Tennessee legislature. But the plea to keep North Carolina from outdoing the state in which the successful movement was launched proved to be effective, and support for matching the $2,000,000 grew rapidly.

Before a bill was introduced in the Tennessee legislature, an agreement was worked out and approved by the North Carolina body whereby a credit of $500,000 would be allowed to Tennessee for having bought the Little River tract of 76,507 acres. On March 30, 1927, Governor Peay announced his approval of another Tennessee bond issue in the amount of $1,500,000. Josephus Daniels,[2] who had become greatly interested in the park, pleaded with Tennessee legislators to act promptly. "It is now or never," he warned.

Knowing that there were those who were honestly opposed to any such state expenditure and that James Wright could be expected to lead the opposition on this new step, the Conservation Association invited Tennessee legislators to make a visit—another for many of them—to the Great Smokies. They accepted, without surprise to anyone, and were brought to Knoxville on a special train for a two-day inspection trip, April 16 and 17. After breakfast at Cherokee Country Club they were taken in cars to the top of the mountain overlooking Cades Cove, where they enjoyed fascinating views as they ate a picnic lunch. Later they were escorted to Mountain View Hotel, Gatlinburg, for a banquet, at which pertinent information was given by park-minded orators. On the following day, three of the hardier or braver guests accepted the invitation for a quick climb of lofty Mt. Le Conte. Others were driven to Elkmont, from which point they returned through the deep-cut gorge of Little River.

On the drive from Gatlinburg to Elkmont they saw roadside signs with the following message: "Inside Park Area: Will Our Homes Be Condemned?" It was not believed that the signs were provided or made by the residents.

Since it would be impractical to buy so much land as was required in this case without the right to condemn any tracts for which the

---

[2] Josephus Daniels was owner-publisher of the *Raleigh News-Observer*. In the Woodrow Wilson administration he was Secretary of the Navy from 1913 to 1921. He served as Ambassador to Mexico for a period of eight years, having been appointed by President Franklin D. Roosevelt in 1933.

asking price was too high, the bill provided for the creation of a commission of seven members with the right of condemnation, a privilege that was to be limited to a period of five years.

Owners of Cherokee Orchard, at the foot of Mt. Le Conte on the Gatlinburg side, and owners of orchards and other property in the vicinity of Elkmont employed John Jennings, a colorful and forceful lawyer of Knoxville, to see that their sections were excluded from condemnation rights—or, if unsuccessful in getting desired amendments inserted, to fight the bill itself. Park leaders, fearing the results of adding Jennings to their foes, agreed to omit the Cherokee Orchard and Elkmont areas—but asked and received permission to have the amendments offered by friends rather than by enemies of the park. As a result, Jennings refused to speak against the bill, leaving Wright to wage his campaign alone.

Used Same Arguments

On the day before the park bill was scheduled for a vote in the House, an anonymous resolution was placed on the desks of the legislators. It urged that they scrap the park movement in favor of a national forest. It quoted a bill which had been introduced in Congress in 1924 by U. S. Senator John K. Shields of Tennessee, providing for the establishment of a national forest in the Great Smokies. It went on to say that there was every reason to believe that a similar bill could be passed when Congress reconvened in December of 1927. A star-boxed insert in the story published in the *Knoxville News-Sentinel* on April 28 read:

The identity of the unknown person whose delayed propaganda for a National Forest, and against a National Park, that was laid on the desks of legislators yesterday was still unknown today, but Postmaster John Waters, of Sevierville, said today that whoever the person was, used the same argument as was used by James Wright, of Knoxville, in a recent conversation with him.

Senator Shields quickly spiked the rumor that he favored a national forest rather than a national park by explaining that his bill, referred to in the anonymous resolution, was drafted prior to the movement for a national park, and that he now favored a national park.

The bill pending in the Tennessee legislature to appropriate $1,500,000 for buying park lands, thus meeting the challenge from the North Carolina legislature, was passed by the Senate on April 21, 1927, by a vote of 23 to 8. Five days later it passed in the House by a vote of 60 to 33, and it was signed the same day by Governor Peay. This was the eighth major accomplishment in the Great Smokies movement.

The bill created a seven-member Tennessee Great Smoky Mountains Park Commission to handle land buying and other phases of the work. Members of the Commission named in the bill were Colonel David C. Chapman, of Knoxville, as chairman; Henry E. Colton, of Nashville; A. E. Markham, of Tiptonville; Ben A. Morton, of Knoxville; Ben W. Hooper, of Newport, succeeded in 1928 by L. S. Allen, also of Newport; E. E. Conner, of Sevierville; and John M. Clark, of Maryville. Their terms of office and their functions were limited to a period of five years, ending in 1932.

Tennessee's $1,500,000 park appropriation was financed by a special gasoline tax of one-tenth of a cent per gallon. North Carolina's $2,000,000 park appropriation bonds were retired by payments from the general state funds.

CHAPTER 8

WHAT'S THE DIFFERENCE?

WHAT IS the difference between a national forest and a national park? This question was asked frequently back in 1924 and is still heard occasionally today. Officers of the Great Smoky Mountains Conservation Association may not have had all the answers when they decided to seek a national park rather than a national forest. In fact, there was some faltering when they made their first decision very early in 1924; but several reasons prompted them to hold firm for a national park, and their determination strengthened greatly as the movement progressed.

Save Virgin Forests

The most important reason was that only through a national park could the vast primeval forests, which covered more than one-third of the Great Smokies, be saved from the lumberman's axe. According to University of Tennessee botanists and National Park Service officials, the Great Smokies contain the nation's largest and finest remaining virgin forest of mixed hardwoods as well as largest and finest forest of virgin red spruce. If this area had become a national forest, much of these stately forests already would have been converted into lumber or pulpwood, with the remainder eventually to meet the same fate. If all of the forest lands of the country had been used for utilitarian purposes, it would have been relatively few decades until the only way by which children could have learned about virgin forests would have been through printed statements and pictures—poor substitutes for the real thing.

National forests are multiple-use areas. Although some of our

Western national forests were created primarily for watershed protection and range management, a major objective for many of the others is to grow trees as a crop, to be harvested at or near maturity. Timber-cutting is carried on carefully and by latest improved methods; but when a single "crop" is sold, the primeval nature of the area is destroyed, and many years pass before a second cutting is ready. Grazing, mining, water-power, and irrigation privileges are granted by sale or lease, hunting and fishing licenses are sold, and sites are leased for summer cottages or year-round occupancy. That is, natural resources are the primary concern, with recreation important, but secondary.

Outdoor Museums

As to the national parks, although fishing is permitted, the seasons and method of fishing are closely regulated. Game animals are given year-round sanctuary, as are all species of flora and fauna, so that park visitors may have the opportunity to see and photograph the animals and plants in their natural habitat, as nearly undisturbed as is reasonably possible. Virgin forests are preserved permanently for their spiritual and aesthetic value to mankind. Children yet unborn will be able to see, study, and enjoy forest areas that remain much as they were when the Pilgrim fathers landed at Plymouth Rock. These majestic areas are outdoor museums which offer soul-stirring adventure and priceless cultural opportunities.

In the early days of the park movement, a few Knoxville citizens believed that a national forest would have a greater commercial value to the communities surrounding the Great Smokies than a national park would have. Park advocates, however, predicted that the national park would soon provide a still greater dollars-and-cents value. After decades of hindsight, it is easy to see that, although the aesthetic facet of the Great Smokies remains the most important consideration, the national park also has a far greater economic value than a national forest could have provided.

A national forest is a high-character commercial enterprise. A national park is essentially a cultural agency, with incidental but important economic benefits. Both national forests and national parks are important conservation branches of the government. Both serve to regulate stream flow, greatly reduce erosion, and reduce floods. Most of the country's publicly owned timber lands are properly included in our national forests. It is tremendously important, however, that such superlative areas as the Great Smokies and other national parks should be preserved undisturbed for all time.

National Parks "Sell" Beauty

National forests sell many things, as has been pointed out. National parks, on the other hand, really have only one "commodity" to "sell"—or, more appropriately, to *give away*. This is the intangible product best described as beauty. It is perhaps the only product or commodity that we can sell and still keep for ourselves. We can sell it again and again, year after year, for endless periods of time, so long as it is protected by national park policies and practices. There are relatively few buyers for some of the things which national forests have for sale. But, fortunately, almost every person now living or yet to be born in this country—not to mention elsewhere— is a potential "buyer" for the beauty that is offered "for sale" in the Great Smokies and other national parks. The millions who each year enjoy these unlimited quantities of beauty derive stimulation for their souls, refreshment for their bodies, and aesthetic enrichment.

Among the most enthusiastic spokesmen for national parks and their functions is David deL. Condon, who has served in many parks.[1] In 1963, while assistant superintendent in the Great Smokies, he referred to the great wealth of natural resources in this park, calling attention to its geology, its varied forms of wildlife, its attractive variety of streams and falls; its "unusual range of plant species," including "some 800 square miles of forested countryside . . . protected and preserved for the 'benefit and enjoyment of the people.'" And, he indicates, in this particular park even those who formerly called the area home are a resource because, in his words, "although their homes are now gone from within its boundaries, [they] have left behind them an aura of mystery and a lore and history of outstanding appeal."

The Smokies, however, he reminds us, is only one of our fine system of national parks, all of which "are utilizing for man's enjoy-

[1] In 1969, assistant superintendent, Grand Canyon National Park.

ment much the same classes of resources"—resources which it is imperative that we protect and preserve under our National Park Service, for, he concludes—emphasizing again the essential difference between national parks and national forests:

Each individual tree is serving mankind in its fullest capacity; it is giving him far greater values than the economics of so many board feet of timber, so many tons of paper pulp, or a given number of dollars as a medium of exchange. Such economic values as these are fleeting and are with man but a short while: he soon spends the money, he moves from the house, he discards the paper products, and he soon burns the logs in his fire. Yes, he needs all of these as part of life, but to be content and happy and to live fully, he needs more. It is this additional something . . . that he gets from the resources perpetuated in their natural state in the National Parks.

These natural resources . . . will, if preserved, continue to give mankind the values of mental relaxation, physical recreation and spiritual stimulation so vital to a happy and full life—those values which are so fleeting and intangible that we can never assess their true value or meaning.

CHAPTER 9

SEARCH FOR A SANTA CLAUS

PASSAGE of the Tennessee bill brought the total park fund to approximately $5,000,000—almost $1,000,000 in private subscriptions and the $2,000,000 each from the two states. It had been felt that this would insure the ultimate success of the movement, but the later and more realistic look showed that much more remained to be done. It was now estimated that a total of $10,000,000 would be required.

Where could the other $5,000,000 be gotten?

For a short time there were thoughts of a nation-wide campaign for funds to be divided between Shenandoah and Great Smokies, but conflicts of interest soon showed such an idea to be impractical. It was next decided that a national campaign for just the Great Smokies would be launched, with Major W. A. Welch—manager of the Palisades Interstate Park and a member of the Southern Appalachian National Park Commission—to head the drive.

Somewhat earlier than this, in October of 1926, when park leaders became aware that "big money" from some outside source would be needed, Henry Ford had been brought for a brief visit to the Great Smokies. He was visiting at nearby Lincoln Memorial University, at Harrogate, Tennessee. A delegation from Knoxville, tactfully driving nothing but Lincoln cars, made an unannounced visit to Harrogate in the hope of inducing the famous industrialist to see the proposed Great Smoky Mountains National Park while he was so near. Mr. Ford at first explained that such a trip was impossible because of earlier commitments. It was a persuasive group, however —possibly aided by the fleet of Lincolns. The result was a visit on the following day. The distinguished guest was taken to Gatlinburg, where he visited the "Pi Phi" school—then operated jointly by the Pi Beta Phi sorority and Sevier County—and talked with Wiley Oakley, "Roamin' Man of the Mountains." Mr. Ford was obviously more attentive to the native wit of Wiley than to information about the proposed park, in which he showed no real interest.

Mrs. Oakley was "expecting" at the time. It soon was an open secret that the next heir in the Oakley household was to be christened "Henry Ford Oakley." Most of the other children had been named for famous and near-famous people whom Wiley had met. The stork apparently got mixed up on the order, however, for he delivered a girl. Not to be outdone, Wiley insisted that the new arrival be called "Mrs. Henry Ford Oakley." Asked later about the health of "Mrs. Henry Ford," Wiley sadly announced, "She died out on me."

The Darkest Hour

But getting back to the efforts to launch a national campaign for Great Smokies funds—from time to time Colonel Chapman reported Major Welch's assurances that the work was getting well under way, with several promises of large subscriptions. He kept a close check on "progress," each time receiving encouraging—but increasingly vague—reports.

Colonel Chapman then reported that it had become more and more difficult to find Major Welch or even to reach him by telephone. Perhaps the darkest hour of the whole movement came on the day when he finally talked with the "leader" of the national campaign, during which the Major admitted that he had not received a single gift and that there was not even a good prospect for one!

Except for the sublime optimism of W. P. Davis, the indomitable fighting spirit of Colonel Chapman, and enthusiastic support from hundreds of faithful co-workers, the movement might have bogged down at this point. Had such a blow come when there was so much skepticism among the workers, it would have been fatal. Fortunately, however, real enthusiasm had long since been generated. Leaders merely dropped the campaign and set to work on other plans for getting the $5,000,000.

It was at this point that big dividends were realized from the friendly relationship that had existed between National Park Service officials and John D. Rockefeller, Jr. Several years earlier Mr. Rockefeller and his young sons had visited national parks in the West. With the gradual development of his interest and personal knowledge of the widespread benefits of these parks to the public, Mr. Rockefeller had provided money here and there for badly needed improvements.

Rockefeller Saves Movement

Realizing that the Great Smokies situation was truly desperate, Director Mather, of the National Park Service, assigned Arno B. Cammerer, associate director, to the task of enlisting the support of Mr. Rockefeller. Cam, as he was affectionately known, had long since become a close personal friend of the noted philanthropist and had occasionally enjoyed the hospitality of the Rockefeller home.

Thus, when he presented the Great Smokies problem, he quickly found a receptive ear. It was soon agreed that, following proper investigation of the whole setup of the Great Smokies movement, a gift of the needed $5,000,000 would be made from the Laura Spelman Rockefeller Memorial—the huge fund established years earlier by John D. Rockefeller, Sr., as a memorial to his wife.

Colonel Chapman and Senator Squires had already been told in strictest confidence of the thrilling news that was to be a lifesaver to the Great Smokies movement. Colonel Chapman often remarked with pride and rejoicing that it had been a most difficult thing to keep such an important secret. He and other park leaders gave complete credit to Mr. Cammerer for obtaining the movement-saving gift; Cam, in turn, gave Colonel Chapman full credit for "selling" Mr. Rockefeller and his staff of investigators on the soundness and honesty of the project and the two park commissions.

Announcement was made simultaneously in Tennessee and North Carolina on March 6, 1928. Kenneth Chorley, representing the Rockefeller Memorial, was present at the Knoxville announcement meeting. He explained the Memorial's readiness to turn over the funds to a board of trustees on a basis of matching, dollar-for-dollar, funds from all other sources. Trustees of the fund were Mr. Cammerer, chairman; Colonel Chapman; and Senator Squires.

This was the ninth major accomplishment in the Great Smokies campaign. Seldom has Knoxville had a day of such intense rejoicing. At four o'clock that afternoon whistles and bells were sounded throughout the city, as news of the vital gift for the park was spread. Although there were possibly as many as a dozen or more steps without which the park could not have been established, this— especially after mature thought—was recognized as the one biggest or most important accomplishment of the whole movement. All the many other big things that had preceded it would have been in vain had not this additional $5,000,000 been received. It was this momentous gift to which reference was made earlier as the reason for requesting the *National Geographic Magazine* to postpone the promised publication of a Great Smokies article.[1] Publicity at this stage would tend to increase land prices, it was feared.

Rockefeller a Conservationist

It is interesting to note, parenthetically, that in March of 1953 Mr. Rockefeller was given an additional "thank-you" through a special twenty-fifth anniversary edition of the *Knoxville Journal*. This was done, also, to let Mr. Rockefeller know that after twenty-five years the people of the region still remembered, with lasting gratitude, his generous gift. Friendly personal letters reminded Mr. Rockefeller that the now-successful Great Smoky Mountains National Park "stands as a living memorial to a wonderful woman," his mother. These brought a warm response from the aging park benefactor.

In one of his letters to the Conservation Association Rockefeller said:

No man ever had a more wonderful mother than I had. The Laura Spelman Rockefeller Memorial Fund was established by my father in her memory. As a trustee of that Fund I was happy to feel that in suggesting a gift of $5,000,000 from it to help in the establishment of the Great Smoky Mountains National Park my mother's name would be memorialized in a way that would be very pleasing to her. You will see, therefore, why I am particularly drawn to your wonderful mountain area.

[1] See Chapter 5.

Over the years, acquaintances in this area came to know something of Rockefeller as a man. His interest in the Great Smokies extended beyond that of financial aid, as was evidenced by a number of visits during the decades after the fund was given. On these trips—always unheralded—he saw something of the mountain people and their way of life, besides enjoying the scenic grandeur. When he stayed over a weekend, it was his habit to attend services at Gatlinburg's First Baptist Church.

On one such visit, made while the Tennessee part of U. S. Highway 441 was being rebuilt, he came in from the North Carolina side. At Newfound Gap he took the chauffeur's place at the wheel, with Mrs. Rockefeller beside him, for the drive down the rugged and highly scenic route to Gatlinburg. A few weeks later he wrote to his close friend, Horace M. Albright, telling of the great enjoyment they had received from that trip to the Great Smokies, especially the drive down "the spectacularly beautiful Tennessee side of the Newfound Gap Highway" and their visit in "the immaculately clean home of Mr. and Mrs. Willie Myers in Cades Cove."

Arthur Stupka, the efficient former Chief Naturalist of the Great Smokies, refers to Rockefeller as a modest man, easily approached, and very sincere and genuine. "On the few occasions when it was my privilege to accompany him on trips through the park I was impressed by his keen interest in the trees of the area," Mr. Stupka once said. Again: "One day, after a tour of the Smokies, the late Robert P. White, then acting superintendent, and I delivered Mr. Rockefeller to the Southern Railway Station in Knoxville. Our attempts to assist him were unavailing, and we watched him descend the long stairway to the train carrying his suitcase. As I recall, he was then in his seventy-sixth year."

When the Great Smokies in 1941 set a new high record for any national park, with more than 1,000,000 visitors in one year, Colonel Chapman sent Mr. Rockefeller a clipping telling about the arrival of the "millionth visitor" of the year. In his reply Rockefeller mentioned the fact that he had "already learned of that important event" through other sources. He then exhibited some more of his modesty as he gave to Colonel Chapman and his fellow workers the main credit for the existence of the park. These are his words:

To you and your associates, whose labors have been crowned with the development of this magnificent park and without whose efforts it would never have come into being, is due the highest credit for its establishment. Please accept my heartiest congratulations on what you have achieved and on this recent evidence of how greatly the park has been used by the people of this country generally. For your kindly reference to the part which the Rockefeller family had in this enterprise, I thank you.

Mr. Rockefeller's interest in national parks dated back at least to 1924, in which year he and his three eldest sons—John, III; Nelson; and Laurance—visited Mesa Verde, Yellowstone and Glacier National Parks. At that time these sons were eighteen, sixteen, and fourteen years old, respectively. Horace M. Albright, then superintendent of Yellowstone National Park, had learned of the approaching visit and took his automobile to Gardiner, Montana, to greet them. He drove to the place where private railroad cars of prominent Yellowstone visitors were parked or "spotted" only to learn that there was no private car on this train. The Rockefellers, traveling under the middle name, Davison, to avoid publicity, had occupied berths on a regular Pullman car.

Albright found the distinguished visitors, introduced himself, and invited them to ride to the hotel in the park automobile. Although Mr. Rockefeller finally accepted for himself, he insisted that his sons ride in the regular public conveyance. Before departing, however, Nelson—later Governor of New York—and Laurance, at their father's suggestion, helped porters move baggage to the Yellowstone bus—not just their own, but that belonging to other park visitors also. John, III, missed the role of assistant porter because, as paymaster of the family group, he was attending to tips for the porters.

Recently, Albright called attention in a personal letter to some of the outstanding evidences of Rockefeller's interest in conserving natural beauty for the public benefit. "Had it not been for Mr. Rockefeller's generosity we would not have had Great Smokies and Grand Teton National Parks. In Grand Teton . . . upwards of $10,000,000 of Rockefeller money has been spent," said Albright. He went on to point out this philanthropist's contribution of $1,750,-000 toward the acquisition of valuable and highly desirable forest lands in Yosemite National Park and his help in financing several other national parks. He bought Linville Falls and a portion of Linville Gorge in North Carolina to be added to the Blue Ridge Parkway and has helped to save several virgin areas of various types in state parks and elsewhere.

"Laurance Rockefeller is carrying on his father's work in conservation," Albright continued. "It was he who bought over 5,000 acres of land on St. John Island in the Virgins and created our 29th National Park. He is chairman of the National Outdoor Recreation Resources Review Commission."

Seek to Collect Pledges

The $5,000,000 Rockefeller gift to the Great Smokies brought the pledged park fund to the needed $10,000,000, thus meeting provisions of both the North Carolina and Tennessee appropriation bills. Governor Henry Horton, who had automatically stepped into office following the death of Governor Peay, notified Governor McLean of North Carolina that, since all necessary funds were then available, he was ready to have Tennessee's bonds issued when notified that North Carolina would take similar action. Two days later, on March 8, 1928, McLean and the North Carolina Council of State approved the issuance of that state's $2,000,000 in bonds.

The life-giving money from the Rockefeller Memorial caused park leaders to realize that a diligent effort must be made to collect the unpaid balances on park pledges. Statements, accompanied by strong appeals for payment, were sent to over eight thousand Tennessee subscribers who still owed part or all of their pledges. Personal calls were made on those with larger balances due. Much money was thus brought in, but there was a substantial total yet to be collected, if possible. Subscribers were reminded that every dollar they paid would give two dollars for land buying, since the Rockefeller money was on a matching basis only, dollar-for-dollar. We were not to get all of the $5,000,000 unless there was an equal amount from other sources. Since the total money actually received from the people and the states of North Carolina and Tennessee fell a little short of the $5,000,000, a small part of the Rockefeller gift was used to match a portion of federal money later allocated.

After numerous appeals for payment and additional statements mailed to subscribers, a number of suits were filed against Tennessee subscribers who had made no effort to pay—or to explain that they could not pay. Practically all of these suits were won by the Conservation Association. The mere fact that action was being brought against some caused others to send in their money. Strangely enough, the one group of exceptions was in Sevier County, the county that was destined to reap the greatest financial harvest from the park. One man there, a county official, admitted that his subscription had been given as "bait," to get others to subscribe, and that he was not expected to pay. Furthermore, he did not pay.

Several others in Sevier County presented a different excuse. They pointed out the wording of the pledge cards, which called for 20 per cent to be paid with the subscription but provided that the other 80 per cent was not due until "the park is established." These delinquent subscribers, represented in the magistrate's court by one of the county's ablest lawyers, insisted that the park had not yet been "established" and that therefore nothing more was due from them. The fact that the first superintendent was already on the job was not recognized by the lawyer or the magistrate as an indication of establishment, and the Sevier County suits were dismissed.

There was another factor, this one altogether legitimate, which militated against the collection of many of the park pledges. It was the big depression of the 1930's, which was already seriously affecting the economy of the region. Many of those who had pledged liberally and in good faith had been forced into bankruptcy, with numerous others tottering on the edge of financial disaster. The depression hampered collections in both states about equally. The fact that North Carolina did not resort to suits in an effort to collect overdue pledges possibly accounts in a large measure for the fact that Tennessee had a considerably better collection record.

Efforts to collect remaining pledges were dropped early in 1933, because so many subscribers simply could not pay. Even so, a few continued to pay voluntarily, but the total amounts were small.

In a letter to Colonel Chapman dated August 10, 1937, National Park Service Director Cammerer gave a final summary of pledges and collections for the two-state fund campaign, as follows:

66

	Amounts Pledged	Amounts Collected	Unpaid Balances as of 5–31–33 [2]
Tennessee	$471,155.09 [3]	$364,681.25 [3]	$106,473.84
North Carolina	397,174.67	147,168.47	250,066.20
Both states	$868,329.76	$511,849.72	$356,540.04

But let us turn our attention for a moment back to the fund-raising campaign and the cards that called for the final 80 per cent when "the park is established." What had been intended, but not clearly stated, was that the final payments would be due when the park seemed assured. Developments revealed that the wording was unfortunate. The psychology of the situation, however, with such an indefinite time for the last payment, worked advantageously in one way. Some subscribers who had been generous had assumed, it seems, that they would never be called upon for the 80 per cent that was deferred. It must be repeated that, even as late as the time of the pledge-taking, many remained extremely doubtful that the project would succeed. Thus, the wording of the pledge cards seems to have conveyed to some that here they could get "credit" for a $5,000 "gift" at an actual outlay of only $1,000, which they felt was going for a good cause—to "advertise Knoxville."

The fund-raising campaign is another instance of success achieved, largely, at least, because a number of persons thought it to be impossible. But, even though much of the money was never collected, the campaign in both states did produce $511,849.72, which was matched from the Rockefeller fund to make a grand total of $1,023,-699.44.

[2] No efforts were made to collect pledges after this date.

[3] The Tennessee totals—for amounts pledged and collected—include $73,000, the appraised value of property given to the park, through the Conservation Association, by Mr. Louis E. Voorhees, a Cincinnati industrialist. Although it was appraised at only $73,000, Mr. Voorhees actually spent over $100,000 on the land, buildings and landscaping. The Voorhees property, containing three homes now used as residences for park officials, is located on Cherokee Orchard Road, near Gatlinburg. Without this gift the Tennessee net pledges would have been $398,155.09, and collections $291,-681.25. The figures for Tennessee do not include Knoxville's one-third of the Little River purchase, which had been listed in the totals at the time of the fund-raising campaign.

CHAPTER 10

LAND BUYING SPEEDED

FOLLOWING receipt of the $5,000,000 Rockefeller gift, the land-buying activities, which up to that time had been limited to small and medium-sized tracts, were greatly accelerated. Preliminary talks were started with owners of the large timber tracts. Surveys were made so that accurate ownership maps could be prepared. On the North Carolina side, with only 401 separate tracts to be bought and with most of the acreage belonging to large timber and pulpwood companies, surveying and mapping were relatively easy in comparison to the work necessitated by more than 6,200 separate properties on the Tennessee side. It is true that approximately 5,000 of these "tracts" were nothing more than small lots in summer colonies and proposed developments. A considerable number of these were 25-foot lots which had been "won" by people who had done nothing more than attend a certain motion picture house. The "gimmick," of course, was that the lucky "winner" would have to buy at least one adjoining lot, as some had done. Such small lots could not be shown separately on a map—even the 12-foot ownership map that was made of the Tennessee side. They did, however, have to be surveyed, and the deeds had to be checked. As already mentioned, it was often as hard to buy a vacant lot or small cottage as to get some of the larger tracts.

In addition to the 5,000 lots, there were slightly more than 1,000 farms on the Tennessee side, many of which extended far up the coves and narrow valleys. Numerous mountain farms had been handed down from generation to generation, with the result that often there was a strong desire to remain at the old home place.

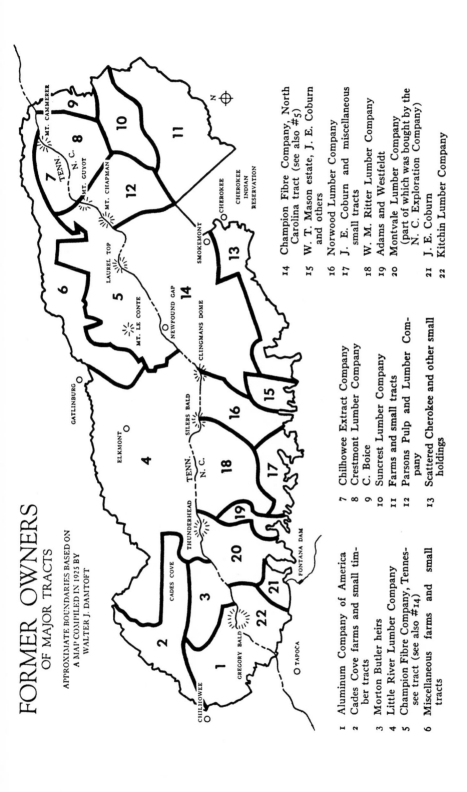

FORMER OWNERS
OF MAJOR TRACTS

APPROXIMATE BOUNDARIES BASED ON
A MAP COMPILED IN 1925 BY
WALTER J. DAMTOFT

1   Aluminum Company of America
2   Cades Cove farms and small tim-
    ber tracts
3   Morton Butler heirs
4   Little River Lumber Company
5   Champion Fibre Company, Tennes-
    see tract (see also #14)
6   Miscellaneous farms and small
    tracts

7   Chilhowee Extract Company
8   Crestmont Lumber Company
9   C. Boice
10 Suncrest Lumber Company
11 Farms and small tracts
12 Parsons Pulp and Lumber Com-
    pany
13 Scattered Cherokee and other small
    holdings

14 Champion Fibre Company, North
    Carolina tract (see also #5)
15 W. T. Mason estate, J. E. Coburn
    and others
16 Norwood Lumber Company
17 J. E. Coburn and miscellaneous
    small tracts
18 W. M. Ritter Lumber Company
19 Adams and Westfeldt
20 Montvale Lumber Company
    (part of which was bought by the
    N. C. Exploration Company)
21 J. E. Coburn
22 Kitchin Lumber Company

This problem, difficult enough at best, was made somewhat easier by an arrangement whereby the owners could sell outright or would be permitted to sell at a reduced figure and retain a lifetime lease. In most cases the expressed longing to remain was based on a genuine wish to do so. In some, however, it was used largely as a bargaining argument, as in one extreme instance in which one of the buyers had been told by adult sons that it would "break the hearts" of their parents if they had to leave. So strong was the plea by the sons that the buyer's only offer was one that would permit the elderly parents to spend their remaining days on the ancestral home place, lest they die of grief. A short time later, when the land-buyer was passing, he was much surprised to see the family in the last stages of moving to a new farm that they had bought in the valley outside the park. When reminded of their eloquent plea not to force "paw and maw" out of their home, the sons admitted that they had long wanted to sell and go where they could make a living more easily, but had never been able to find a buyer. This is an appropriate place for a comment that, although most of them have little formal education, the mountain people had a well-earned reputation for being shrewd traders.

Other kinds of problems also rose. For instance, mapping and checking deeds for many tracts of land was made extremely difficult by the rather general practice of describing boundaries by reference to vague or non-permanent "markers." The writer's daughter, Jean —now Mrs. H. C. Harvey, Jr.—in 1935 was assigned the subject of "History of Cades Cove" as her high-school history term paper. One of her sources of information was abstracts of park deeds, then available in the office of the Park Commission in Knoxville, but later stored safely away in the Interior Department Building, in Washington. Among these abstracts were many descriptions of boundaries that could scarcely be followed or even located a few years after they were written. In one deed one side of the property followed the stream "down to where an old sow swam the river." Another followed a certain road from an established corner "to the fifth row of corn." Reminiscent of the fact that Indians had lived in the vicinity not so many years earlier, some of the deeds referred to "corner trees" that bore a specified number of tomahawk marks. Not all deeds were so carelessly described, of course. Many used the orthodox "metes and bounds" of the surveyors and civil engineers. But another type of confusion is illustrated by a deed that contained an affidavit from Andy Gregory, the famous mountain surveyor. Gregory told that, because of insanity that was rather prevalent among the heirs of a deceased landowner—citing them by name and degree of insanity—they could not execute a legal deed. This is one of the cases later referred to by Colonel Chapman when he told legislators that the Park Commission would need the right to condemn even if there was no argument as to the price to be paid.

Roads or Park?

It must be recalled that just prior to the launching of the park movement there had been a general clamor in Knoxville and nearby communities, and on the North Carolina side, for a road across the mountains, a commercial road. Nobody ever mentioned the fact that such a road would open up vistas of unbelievable grandeur and beauty. Most of the men who later became park leaders were active at first in this campaign for a trans-mountain road; but, as the park project reached the land-buying stage, these same men now concentrated on trying to delay the road building. The reason is obvious: construction of such a road would inescapably bring an increase in the prices asked for remaining lands.

Some Sevierville leaders, however, frankly admitted that they would rather have the road than the park, possibly still believing that the latter would never be a reality. They chided their former fellow road boosters. Governor Peay was caught in the middle of the argument. He held off as long as he felt that he could, but finally gave in to the road advocates, especially those who wanted a route through the center of the park. As first planned, it was to cross at Indian Gap—at the point where the old Indian Road had crossed, and about the only spot known to most of them. In fact, the project was referred to as the Indian Gap Highway even for some time after engineers found that a better grade could be gotten by crossing at Newfound Gap, a mile and a half farther east.

In spite of park leaders' warnings that any road that the state would build would almost surely not meet national park standards and therefore would have to be rebuilt later, the road enthusiasts

71

won. A contract awarded by the Tennessee Highway Department in July, 1927, was completed in the summer of 1929, the contract price being $324,388. North Carolina road officials, meantime, cooperated more closely with their park officials and delayed for a while, not completing their part of the highway until the summer of 1930.

The prediction that a state road would not meet park standards was thoroughly justified. In a brief few years, in the mid-thirties, the National Park Service found it necessary to reconstruct the upper three-fourths of the Tennessee side, at a cost of $1,250,000. The new road included two tunnels and a "loop-over" so as to eliminate some of the dangerously sharp curves. The lower portion was likewise rebuilt, somewhat later, at an additional cost, to correct the narrowness and crookedness of the state-built road. The upper five miles on the North Carolina side, which was dangerously steep in addition to having continuous sharp curves, was being rebuilt in 1960 on an entirely new location, at an estimated cost of $2,500,000.

Little River Tract Again

The whole park movement was amazingly complex. There was hardly a period when there were not at least two activities demanding immediate attention. The Little River Lumber Company tract is a case in point; it had a way of creating crises at unexpected times and in unpredictable ways—as it did in 1927, simultaneously with the complications over the road.

When Governor Peay, in March of 1927, delivered the state's check to Colonel Townsend and in return received the deed for the land—following the dismissal of an injunction on the previous day— it was confidently believed by most people that this was now a closed matter. But not so. In January of 1928 another injunction seeking a refund of the money that had been paid was before the Tennessee Supreme Court. This new injunction effort accomplished nothing for foes of the park, but it had to be fought by park and state attorneys.

Still another, more serious, problem arose. Reports of widespread "slashing" in the Little River timber cutting were heard. Terms of the sale agreement permitted cutting of trees over ten inches in diameter, but the company was charged with a type of operation that virtually destroyed smaller timber. Upon investigation, however, Colonel Chapman and members of the park staff reported finding relatively little damage in a few small areas. Nevertheless, the Park Commission considered buying the remaining timber rights but felt the price of $1,250,000 prohibitive, especially since the park's timber cruisers reported only about one-sixth as much standing timber as had been claimed and since, furthermore, the 1927 appropriation of $1,500,000 from Tennessee carried a provision that none of that money could be used for timber rights. Although the Park Commission had other funds available, it now considered abandoning efforts to buy the standing timber "because there was so little of it."

The *News-Sentinel*, however, waged a continued campaign seeking to stop what it classed as ruthless destruction. In May of 1928 and again in February of 1929 that park-minded newspaper published full-page stories, with numerous photographs made on the scene by its own photographers. The pictures, and the editorialized stories accompanying them, revealed real desolation. Colonel Townsend protested that the pictures were made at spots where there had been unusually dense stands of large trees, with no room for smaller trees under them.

Secretary Work had already warned that the federal government would not accept land for park purposes if timber cutting was permitted, and at this juncture Rockefeller officials announced that they were greatly disturbed by the reports, explaining that it was largely to save the virgin forests that their money had been given. When it came time to deed the Little River tract to the federal government, the papers had to be redrawn so as to eliminate the lower portion of the Middle Prong watershed, on which cutting privileges were still outstanding. The Park Service would not accept the land with such restrictions.

In February of 1929 Colonel Townsend published appeals for understanding on the part of Knoxville businessmen, citing the fact that his company had monthly payrolls of from $25,000 to $30,000, most of which eventually reached Knoxville merchants. The *News-Sentinel* reminded that such payrolls were to continue for only a few years at the longest, but that the park would grow in value to the same merchants from year to year.

Park leaders endeavored to get a bill through the 1929 legislature giving the Park Commission the right to condemn the remaining timber. Because of strong opposition from various sources, however, and an adverse report of the legislative committee to which it had been referred, the bill was withdrawn. In its vigorous fight for this bill, the *News-Sentinel* had again and again intimated that failure of passage might make it impossible to stop the timber cutting (especially the "ruthless methods" being practiced) and might even kill the whole park project. But the *Knoxville Journal,* in an editorial on February 8, 1929, disagreed, stating that "neither the passage nor the defeat of the bill to condemn the timber rights will destroy the park movement. . . . The Great Smoky Mountains Park movement is bigger than any lumber company, any group of men, any individual or any newspaper." It accused the *News-Sentinel* of hysteria.

The Park Commission did salvage some of the uncut timber acreage. It gave up an unwanted tract of land near Kinzel Springs in exchange for some 65 acres at Elkmont, eight steel bridges—all of which were needed—and the release of timber rights on approximately 3,300 acres of land. This exchange was cited during a later legislative investigation as a bad trade for the park, but Secretary Ickes considered it advantageous. What had actually happened was this: the Commission had paid $150,000 for an estimated 51,000,-000 board feet of virgin timber; and it had saved a strip eight miles long and 660 feet wide (by level measurement, but a much greater distance by surface measurement) on the main crest or state line.

Looking ahead a few years, we see that on October 11, 1935, the Little River Company released all rights to 17,000 acres of land from which the timber recently had been cut, so that it could be deeded in fee to the federal government by the Park and Forestry Commission. This left relatively little more land on which the company could still remove standing timber. The last cutting by the Little River Lumber Company was on the Spruce Flats Branch early in 1938, which was a few years before the company's deadline date for cutting.

It is regrettable, of course, that not all of the virgin timber on the Little River tract could have been saved. But the "silver lining" to this dark cloud lies in the fact that it is here, where there was so much desolation and ugliness following lumbering operations, that park visitors of later years have found the brightest and most abundant autumn colors. Several times each October, autumn color caravans also go to upper Little River, in the Tremont section, where the

Little River Lumber Company removed the timber by the same methods.

The North Carolina Situation

During approximately the same period, the North Carolina Commission was proceeding with land purchases, but the state money was threatened as a result of the litigation with Suncrest Lumber Company, one of the large landowners of that state. The company's suit, which, among other matters, questioned the legality of the state's appropriation bill, was dismissed in August, however. In January, 1929, Chief Justice William Howard Taft of the U. S. Supreme Court, ruled that the act, as passed by the 1927 legislature, was legal.

Early in March the Commission announced the purchase of the Norwood tract of 17,063 acres at a cost of $86,320. This land, which had been logged several years earlier and on which there had been extensive forest fires in 1925, is in the Forney Creek watershed and comes up to the state line from Clingmans Dome to Silers Bald.[1]

---

[1] It is encouraging to see the dense stands of vigorous young red spruce, with trees already twenty or more feet high in 1960, growing both above and below the end of the road at Clingmans Overlook, near the summit of Clingmans Dome.

75

CHAPTER 11

ACCUSATIONS
INSTEAD OF THANKS

NEW and ominous clouds appeared as park leaders were preparing for the introduction of a bill in the 1929 legislature of Tennessee, seeking to extend the boundaries in which the commission had the right to condemn land for the park. The bill was to exclude Gatlinburg and Kinzel Springs (Sunshine), but was to include Elkmont, Wonderland Park, Cherokee Orchard, and Pittman Center. Two days before this bill was to have been introduced, another, presented in both houses, called for a full-scale investigation of the activities of the Park Commission. Still another, sponsored by foes of the park leaders, provided for enlargement of the Park Commission. This last-named bill was construed as an effort to oust Colonel Chapman as chairman, to "force" the Rockefeller money to be turned over to the state (as if that could have been done!), and likewise to "force" the Conservation Association to turn its funds over to the state (an action which might or might not have been possible).

A political column written by a staff member of the *Nashville Tennessean,* and for a period also published in the *Knoxville Journal,* regularly sniped at Colonel Chapman in particular and the Chapman-influenced Commission in general. In one of these columns there was reference to "the bull-headed idiocy of the Chapman policy." In another the columnist audaciously called for Chapman's resignation. The *Nashville Banner* was also extremely critical of the park movement, particularly the purchase of the Little River Lumber Company tract.

Officials of the Laura Spelman Rockefeller Memorial wired Gov-

ALUM CAVE BLUFF: Getting around this spectacular bluff was a real problem for the first two members of Dr. Work's committee. It is now a popular destination for hikers.

—*Jim Thompson*

HUGGINS HELL: The rugged section pictured below formerly belonged to Champion Fibre Company. It is typical of the "rolling land" owned by that company.

—*Jim Thompson*

—*Jim Thompson*

RUGGEDNESS: This view from Chimney Tops shows some of the "ruggedness of of the area" mentioned by Dr. Work's committee. Newfound Gap Highway, U. S. 441, winds through Sugarland Valley below. The entrance to Chimneys Campground is at the lower left.

ernor Horton in protest of the rumored plans to remove Colonel Chapman. Many Knoxville and other East Tennessee citizens and organizations bombarded the Governor and members of the legislature in behalf of the park leader. Advocates of the bill to enlarge the Commission claimed that the purpose of the measure was to add "businessmen" to the group, clearly implying that the body was lacking in that respect. To this the *News-Sentinel* replied by citing the top-ranking business stature of Colonel Chapman, Mr. Morton, and other members of the existing Commission.

The bill did not pass. In fact, efforts to work up sentiment for it were dropped. But the park enemies had not given up. They merely attacked from another direction, campaigning successfully for the proposed legislative investigation.

This investigation started in Knoxville on February 28, 1929. The Tennessee Commission was accused of illegally lending $250,000 of Tennessee money to the North Carolina Commission. Colonel Chapman explained that it was Rockefeller, not Tennessee, money that had been advanced to the North Carolina body, and that it was done so that the sister group could proceed with condemnation action against owners of large tracts. He further explained that the Rockefeller money was not designated for 50-50 division between the two states, but was to be used where most needed. These candid explanations caused several "charges" to be dropped quickly. One of these was the charge that Colonel Chapman had made numerous trips to New York at the expense of the Commission. This he most satisfactorily disposed of when he explained that most of the trips were made in connection with the successful effort to obtain the $5,000,000 Rockefeller gift.

The *News-Sentinel* of March 5 quoted the chairman of the investigating committee as saying, "The man who was responsible for the legislative investigation of the State Park Commission will be given an opportunity this afternoon to produce his evidence." The *Journal* of the next morning reported that this man, James B. Wright, had refused to submit affidavits [1] unless he could do so in executive session. It added that Colonel Chapman had been assured that members of

---

[1] Mr. Wright later published the affidavits and other anti-park information in book form. Copies were given to members of the legislature.

the Park Commission would be allowed to hear and cross-examine the witness. Mr. Wright was quoted as admitting that there had been no dishonesty on the part of park officials, but as insisting that the Conservation Association should have been made to turn over its funds to the Commission. Colonel Chapman gave several satisfactory reasons why such would have been unwise at the time.

The Colonel was also asked why so much time had been spent buying small and relatively unimportant tracts instead of buying such tracts as that of the Champion Fibre Company. He explained that the Commissions of the two states could not deal intelligently with the Champion tract until they knew as much about the company's property as did the owners.[2]

Another question had to do with the expense of the special train that had brought members of the legislature to Knoxville in 1927 for a visit to the Great Smokies. Ben W. Hooper, ex-governor and former member of the Park Commission, inquired about various expenses of the trip. After an accounting that included cost of the special trains, banquet, and hotel bills, Mr. Hooper asked what had been bought with the difference. "Just such things as members of the legislature wanted," Colonel Chapman replied, amid laughter from most of those present.

Thus, the investigation was based on a few serious charges, which were shown to be wholly without foundation, and on others of a trivial or gossipy nature, apparently intended to embarrass Colonel Chapman.

On April 15 a majority report of the investigating committee was submitted to the legislature. It praised the work of Colonel Chapman and other members of the Park Commission, made special mention of the fact that the records had been kept in a businesslike manner, and contained special thanks to the Rockefeller Memorial for its gift to the Great Smokies.

Colonel Chapman modestly admitted to close friends that, when he went with other park leaders to the legislature seeking the extension of condemnation privileges, he had confidently expected the bill to be passed quickly, possibly with a "vote of appreciation" for the work that had been done. He added that it had come, therefore,

[2] This important property is dealt with in Chapter 12.

as a stunning blow to be turned down on the condemnation bill and instead be forced to undergo such investigation as that which he had just been through.

As these instances illustrate only too well, park opponents took advantage of every conceivable opportunity to hamper the progress of the movement or to harass those who worked for it. Some even went so far as to embarrass a representative of the Rockefeller Memorial, or to place him in a compromising position, by offering unsolicited and unwanted "courtesies" of a questionable nature. Such annoyances continued right up to the termination of the long struggle, as subsequent chapters show.

CHAPTER 12

THE VERY HEART OF THE PARK

EVEN BEFORE receipt of the Rockefeller gift, members of the
Park Commissions of the two states held preliminary conferences
with Reuben B. Robertson, president of Champion Fibre Company,
relative to the purchase of that company's tract of 92,814.5 acres.
This constitutes by far the largest tract in the park, but equally important is the fact that it is the very heart of the park, including all
or part of the several highest peaks of the Smokies and the nation's
finest stands of virgin red spruce and virgin mixed hardwoods. It includes part of Clingmans Dome and part of Mt. Guyot—the two
highest peaks of the Smokies; all of Mt. Le Conte, Chimney Tops,
the extremely rugged section of the main crest called Sawtooth
Range; the Greenbrier wilderness area, on the Tennessee side; and
the Three Forks wilderness area, on the North Carolina side. Most
of the really big trees of the Smokies, several of which are the largest
known trees of their respective species, grow on the Champion Fibre
tract.

On December 7, 1925, the Champion Fibre Company published a
full-page advertisement in Knoxville newspapers in which it expressed "admiration and respect" for sponsors of the national park,
"who are so generously giving their time, efforts and money to the
furtherance of their program." It went on to extend "profound regret
that we find ourselves at variance with them in judgment as to the
best course to follow." It then indicated preference for a national
forest, explaining that the company favored more tourists, but also
favored industrial activities.

Returning from a Champion Fibre conference in October of 1926,
Colonel Chapman stated that he expected the purchase of that tract

to be consummated with a "minimum of complications." Shortly afterwards, however, there developed a considerable difference of opinion which the park people had not anticipated. Mr. Robertson let it be known that the company's huge pulp mill at Canton, North Carolina, had been built primarily to handle the spruce which the company had bought in the Great Smokies. He explained that both the mill and the company's railroad lines already built into parts of their Great Smokies tract must be bought along with the timber land. The surprised park leaders insisted that—since the mill and much of the railroad in question were several miles from the timber land—these items should not be considered.

Already the situation was rather obviously something more than the "minimum of complications" that Colonel Chapman had anticipated. As the Colonel had explained to the investigating committee, it had been the tremendous differences of opinion on value of the property that had prompted the Commissions to postpone talks with Mr. Robertson and wait till they had more money and more knowledge of the property involved.

It was only after receipt of the Rockefeller gift that park leaders resumed negotiations for the Champion Fibre property. But the wide differences in valuation still appeared irreconcilable. It became obvious that some third party would have to be brought into the negotiations. During a meeting in November, 1929, Mr. Robertson suggested that arbitration be used, but the Commissions doubted that they had the right to bind themselves to a decision reached by that method. Park officials suggested an alternative: that condemnation suits be filed, with the understanding that, if it should later become possible to do so, they could agree on a price and drop the legal action. At the close of that conference Colonel Chapman announced that his group's suggestion was to be used, by agreement of both sides; but Mr. Robertson denied having agreed to anything other than arbitration. Thus, the meeting that was first announced as successful turned out a complete failure.

Next, both state Commissions decided that condemnation was the only course open to them. Members of the Tennessee Commission asked the North Carolina body to file proceedings first because North Carolina's condemnation laws were "more favorable" than Tennessee's. But when the North Carolina group made no move to act, the Tennesseans began extensive preparations for filing a suit in circuit court in Sevierville, Tennessee.

Recalling Colonel Chapman's statement, already mentioned, that no negotiations could be concluded with Champion Fibre officials until the two Commissions knew "as much about their property as they do" gives some clue as to how extensive the preparations for that condemnation suit were to be. Experienced timber cruisers were employed, largely on the basis of their established reputations in that work and the prestige they would take with them to the witness stand. These men were sent into the field to see how much usable timber there was, what was the nature or topography of the land on which it was growing, and how the timber could be gotten from there to the company's mill at Canton, North Carolina. They also employed several of the leading paper-pulp engineers, industrial engineers, foresters, and railroad contractors of the United States and Canada.

With the technical information of those internationally famous experts at their command, the Tennessee Commission on January 1, 1930, filed its condemnation suit against the Champion Fibre Company. Some six weeks later the company filed a demurrer. Actual trial of the case was started on November 17, 1930, with the selection of a five-man jury of view. Since the attorneys for the Park Commission were from Nashville and Knoxville, they had to have the help of Sevierville attorneys, who were better acquainted with Sevier County citizens. These local attorneys sat with the Commission's counsel both during the selection of the jury and during other phases of the case. The jury of view consisted of C. A. Temple, J. C. Cole, C. L. Thurman, Ashley Large, and J. H. Denton. The purpose of the suit was to buy the 39,549 acres that lay on the Tennessee side, all in Sevier County, the assessed value of these holdings being only $323,500.

Company witnesses, presumably equal in experience and reputation to those of the Park Commission, testified that the land in question was worth from $4,000,000 up to $7,000,000. The company's spruce timber was described accurately, it is believed, as the "finest in the country, both in size of trees and density of tree growth." One witness for the company admitted on cross-examination, however, that he did not know the current value of spruce wood.

Mr. Robertson stated that the big mill at Canton had been located and built at that point only because of the company's extensive spruce holdings in the Great Smokies. He added that, if the land were to be taken from them, the mill and its connecting railroads would have to be closed, as would the company's smaller mill at Smokemont, North Carolina, inside the park area, where cutting had already been in progress. Company witnesses admitted, on cross-examination, that elaborate preparations would have to be made to get out the timber on the Tennessee side and move it across the mountain to a mill in North Carolina. An official of the company said that $1,700,671 had already been invested in the Tennessee tract. Of this, $643,519 was listed as the original purchase price back in 1917–1919, with such items as interest and cost of patrolling running it up to the $1,700,671 figure. A ripple of laughter swept through the crowded courtroom when one of the company witnesses referred to the property as "rolling land." "Rolling land" is a term generally used in eastern Tennessee and western North Carolina to describe land that is not level but is sufficiently gentle of slope to permit the use of farm machinery in its cultivation.

Much of the Commission's testimony dealt with the extreme ruggedness of the area—the roughest in the whole park—the expense of building railroads for removal of the timber, and the allegedly low cost of bringing in pulpwood from Canada and Russia. One Commission witness testified that it would cost $3,000,000 just to build the necessary railroads. Another placed this expense at $1,200,000. A company witness had estimated it at only $600,000. Commission witnesses valued the property at from $300,000 to $800,000. A Commission witness, who claimed thirty years of experience in that field, testified that it would cost $19.98 per cord just to remove the wood and transport it to the North Carolina mill. He quoted a Champion Fibre wood-buyer as then paying only $18 per cord for wood delivered to the mill, thus implying that the timber on the Tennessee side was actually worthless to the company.

Value—$2,550,000

The North Carolina Supreme Court had ruled, in the Suncrest Lumber Company case, that owners of timber lands in the park area are entitled to "incidental damages" for their mills and railroads, even though those properties might be outside the park area. The Tennessee Commission had argued, nevertheless, that Champion's land in Tennessee was very different because of the greater distance between the timber and the mill and the separation of the two by high and rugged mountains, those factors rendering the timber on the Tennessee side of no value to the company's mill at Canton.

The trial lasted a total of seventeen days, with the Commission using eight of them and the company the other nine. The jury of view was unable to agree on a price that all would recommend, and a divided verdict was submitted on January 16, 1931. The majority, three of the five members, placed the value of the land and timber at $2,325,000, with another $225,000 as "incidental damages" for the company's mill and railroad, or a total verdict of $2,550,000 for the 39,549 acres. C. A. Temple and C. L. Thurman, the minority members of the jury, valued land and timber at $1,250,000 with no "incidental damages."

Colonel Chapman announced the majority verdict as a "stunning blow" to the park and said that, if that verdict were allowed to stand, it would kill the park movement. He predicted that the Commission would take a "nonsuit," or appeal to a jury of twelve in circuit court. A week later the case was appealed.

A conference between Commission members from both states and Fibre Company officials was held just after the termination of the condemnation suit, but by agreement there was no announcement of the discussions that took place.

Many years later, on September 11, 1958, this writer had a conference in Asheville, North Carolina, with Mr. Robertson, chairman of the board of the current company, and Walter J. Damtoft, recently retired chief forester for the company.[1] During this interview Mr. Damtoft, a long-time acquaintance of the writer, produced longhand notes that he made at the time.

The Damtoft notes stated that the purpose of the 1931 conference was to try for a compromise purchase of the Tennessee land. Mr. Robertson was asked to name a figure that he would accept, to which he replied $4,000,000, with a comment that considerable money had

---

[1] Robertson and Damtoft are the only surviving principals of the 1931 conference in Sevierville.

THE VERY HEART OF THE PARK

recently been spent—apparently referring to the cost of the Sevierville trial and the preparations for it.

Colonel Chapman was quoted as having said that he had had recent information, apparently later than the testimony of the Commission witnesses, from high authorities that had caused him to
change his views. He went on to say that the maximum figure that
the Commissions would entertain would now be less than the *$3,250,-
000 which had been previously offered* and refused.[2] As he started to
name the maximum figure they would consider, Robertson inter-
rupted to state that the "irreducible minimum" was $3,250,000.
Chapman replied that it would be of no use to mention a figure of
even one-half that amount; whereupon Robertson indicated that he
would submit to his board of directors "any serious offer" that the
park would make, but would make no promise as to what the action
of the board might be.

To this, the Colonel responded that the Commissions were in a
position to offer $1,500,000.

"For the Tennessee portion?" Mr. Robertson asked.

"No, for the entire boundary," Colonel Chapman replied.

Mr. Damtoft's notes state that at that point Mr. Robertson "blew
his top," declaring that he would not think about submitting such a
ridiculous figure to his board.

The conference was then adjourned, with a suggestion from Mr.
Morton that a further study be made by both sides.

At the 1958 interview, Robertson and Damtoft stated that Morton
had taken a pacifying role throughout the conference. They made
no further reference to Colonel Chapman's part in the lively discussions. It was a known fact that friction between the forceful park
leader and the equally dynamic Robertson had been developing for
some time prior to those discussions.

Attention was called to the purchase by the North Carolina Commission of 20,229 acres from Crestmont Lumber Company for only
$5.50 per acre. That tract, in the Big Creek watershed, heading
up to Mt. Guyot, adjoins the Champion Fibre tract for a distance
of a mile along the state line.

[2] That figure, which had never been made public, was $250,000 more than the
eventual purchase price for Champion's land in *both states.*

In a letter to Colonel Chapman, which was published in several newspapers, including the *Asheville Times* of January 23, 1931, Mr. Robertson stated that at the request of park leaders Champion had stopped timber cutting on its property three years earlier, and that it had been done in the belief that the two Commissions were trying to establish the park at the earliest possible date, that they would treat his company fairly, and that they would make an effort to arrive at a fair price. He further stated that the company did not want to put any obstacles in the way of the park, although it meant a sacrifice to give up a large part of the property that had been acquired to safeguard a future supply for the mill.

"I felt that we should make the sacrifice in the public good, provided we were paid the reasonable value of the property," Robertson wrote. Recalling that he had previously suggested arbitration as a means of arriving at a fair price for the land, he added, "You elected to take your case to court, which was your right. The jury rendered its verdict. I now observe from the newspapers that you are making what I consider a very unfair attack upon the verdict."

In his reply to that letter Colonel Chapman said, "I realize that delays have been annoying and expensive to you." But, he pointed out, the unavoidable delays were also costing the respective states many thousands of dollars. Reviewing the fact that the testimony of the Commission's eleven witnesses put the average valuation at $555,455, Chapman added, "I have been told many times in western North Carolina that you stopped cutting spruce on your land because the costs were prohibitive and not because the park came into the picture."

At numerous points in this disturbing controversy, park leaders expressed fear that the Rockefeller money might be recalled because of the Champion Fibre case.

In March of 1931 the company retained John W. Davis [3] as an additional member of its already strong legal staff. On March 27 a conference was started in the Washington offices of the National Park Service. Attending were members of both Park Commissions; members of the National Park Service staff, including Director Al-

[3] John W. Davis, famous Ohio lawyer, was the Democratic candidate for President in 1924, having run against Calvin Coolidge.

bright and Associate Director Cammerer; Secretary of the Interior Ray Lyman Wilbur; and officials of the Champion Fibre Company.

Prior to this Washington conference, however, Robertson and Davis had sought to get Albright to arbitrate the Tennessee side of the case. "I remember that I felt highly honored but nevertheless uneasy to sit and listen while those great men stood before me arguing their case," Mr. Albright recalled some years later. "I was uneasy because I knew that I had to give them a negative answer, which I did. I could not let myself get in the position of arbitrator between such adversaries as the Champion Fibre Company and the State of Tennessee. Davis and Robertson argued with me all morning trying to get me to see their point of view and accede to their request. Of course, as I told them, it is probable that the Tennessee Commission would have rejected me."

Mr. Albright was much too modest. Had the Tennessee leaders felt that they had authority to fix values by arbitration—which they did not—they would have been glad to have a man of Albright's unquestioned integrity and ability to serve as the third party.

After the arbitration efforts failed, Messrs. Robertson and Davis agreed to participate in the Washington conference. Early in the discussions Robertson submitted the $3,250,000 price—not at the time announced publicly, but revealed at the September, 1958, conference. Park leaders considered it to be much too high.

Reports at the time indicate that the Chapman-Robertson friction again became very apparent, with the result that the conference almost ended before it got well started. So heated were some of the exchanges between these opponents that it was decided to put members of the two Park Commissions in one room and Champion Fibre officials in another. Park Service staff members Albright and Cammerer served as "messengers," carrying comments, proposals and counterproposals from one group to the other. This went on into the third day, with little hope in sight at any time. On the third day, however, an agreement was reached, the whole 92,814.5 acres being bought at the price of $3,000,000. Although the agreement did not allocate the purchase price, the two Commissions decided that North Carolina should pay $2,000,000 for the 53,265.5 acres in that state and Tennessee should pay $1,000,000 for its 39,549 acres. Thus,

Tennessee got for $1,000,000 the land which a majority of the jury of view had valued at $2,550,000.

Tennessee paid an average of $25.28 per acre, whereas North Carolina paid an average of $37.55 per acre. The average paid for the entire tract, in both states, was $32.33 per acre. The difference paid per acre by the two states was due to the fact that the North Carolina tract was much closer to the company's mill than was the land on the Tennessee side. The $32.33 per acre average paid for the Champion Fibre land is higher than the average for the whole park because most of this tract was, and still is, a virgin forest.

This negotiated purchase of the Champion Fibre tract caused great rejoicing among park enthusiasts on both sides of the mountains. An Asheville spokesman heralded it as the biggest news for western North Carolina in the forty years that he had lived there. As Colonel Chapman and Mr. Morton alighted from the train in Knoxville, on their return from the successful parley in Washington, they were given a typical heroes' welcome. The Knoxville High School Band was there, as was a large delegation of elated park workers. Following a rousing reception at the station, the joyful throng paraded through the downtown section.

This immediate and natural rejoicing was followed shortly by some sober warnings from park leaders and newspapers. They urged that land speculation, which had been going on in some places, be stopped and that no further buying for profit be allowed in any part of the park area. Much land was still to be bought. If the limited amount of money was to complete the job, a fair level of prices, free from padding, would have to be maintained. The Knoxville Chamber of Commerce announced that it would take steps seeking to prevent such obstruction of the park project.

Titles Cleared

In checking the deeds for the Champion tract, the park legal staff had to examine the "claims" of 444 persons who had at least thought they owned parts of the property. The unnamed heirs of Radford Gatlin were among them. Mr. Gatlin, a brother of the inventor of the famous Gatlin gun, had owned extensive lands in the Smokies at the time of the Civil War, when he was literally run out of the area

88

by Union sympathizers because of his expressed Confederate sentiments. Gatlinburg, headquarters city for the park, was later renamed for Mr. Gatlin. It had formerly been known as White Oak Flats.

The 67-page deed to the Tennessee side of the property was delivered to Colonel Chapman and other park officials in Knoxville on May 9, 1931, by Mr. Robertson. As he made the presentation, he stated that he was glad that the company's land, so ideally suited to park purposes, was to be a part—the very heart, in fact—of the park. He had already delivered to Senator Squires and other North Carolina park workers the deed to the land in that state.

New Light on an Old Subject

As had been the case with the Little River Lumber Company tract, where timber-cutting rights brought new problems after it was thought that the case was closed, the Champion Fibre condemnation suit was brought back into the limelight some five years later by a development of a surprising nature. The Bureau of Internal Revenue, as the Internal Revenue Service was then called, in checking the 1931 income tax returns of the Champion Fibre Company, learned that two payments totaling $15,000 had been made to D. Clyde Bogart, a Sevierville attorney who had previously been employed by the Tennessee Park Commission to help select a jury of view in the Champion Fibre case. Court records show that the payments to Bogart were made by Charles C. Benedict, an attorney of Cincinnati, Ohio, through the use of checks executed by Champion Fibre Company payable to himself and endorsed by him to Bogart.[4] The information was brought out during the progress of a disbarment suit which was filed against Bogart on October 2, 1935, by Sevier County Magistrate Conley Huskey.[5] Bogart was "suspended from practicing law in all courts of this State for a period of five years. . . ."[6]

In his circuit court judgment Judge W. P. Monroe included the following statement: "The result was that the trial before the jury of

---

[4] *Civil Minutes 4,* p. 510, Office of the Circuit Court Clerk, Sevierville, Tennessee.
[5] *Ibid.*
[6] *Ibid.,* p. 530.

view selected by an attorney accepting employment from the plaintiff and the defendant in the same case could be nothing more than a sham battle and a clear mockery of justice." [7] Judge Monroe also held that the defendant, as charged, had said to a prospective juror, "I may want a high or a low verdict." [8]

[7] *Ibid.*, p. 511.
[8] *Ibid.*, p. 510.

CHAPTER 13

THE CHAMPION FIBRE CASE
IN RETROSPECT

THE Champion Fibre case developed some points of high drama. On the one hand was the park group, men who had experienced some surprising obstacles, trying desperately and with limited funds to establish a national park. On the other hand was an industrialist who was trying to protect the large investments of his company. As one looks back at the fight as objectively as possible, it seems that a project of such magnitude, with so much at stake on both sides, would almost inevitably bring a clash of personalities and attendant personal animosities. It also seems that the passage of time would tend to erase or soften the harshness and bitterness that was present in "the heat of battle."

To a certain extent this change was evidenced not very many months after the close of the case when, on December 13, 1932, Mr. Robertson wrote to Senator Squires, chairman of the North Carolina Commission, in this vein:

You and your commission have engaged on a task which holds much hope for the advancement of western North Carolina. It so happened that the project threatened to disturb the favorable position of our particular industry. Whatever the ultimate effect upon us may be we shall nevertheless rejoice as citizens of western North Carolina if the general welfare is enhanced.

The fact that no such letter was written to Colonel Chapman is easily understood in view of the numerous clashes of interest between the two men, whereas no North Carolina Commission member was engaged in such a conflict.

As this book was in preparation, however, the writer could not refrain from wondering what Mr. Robertson's views were after the passage of three decades. With such thoughts in mind he sought and obtained the previously mentioned conference with Mr. Robertson for a backward look. This conference, during some parts of which Mr. Damtoft was also present, was held on September 11, 1958, as stated earlier. It was followed by letters from Mr. Robertson in which he put in writing the information he had given orally.

At the outset Robertson gave National Park Service Director Albright full credit for conceiving and arranging the all-important 1931 Washington conference. A letter from Albright to John W. Davis shortly after Davis was retained by the Fibre Company led to the conference. Robertson stated that Davis had been brought into the case in the hope that he could help to avoid further litigation, but with the realization that, if the case should be carried to the U. S. Supreme Court, the company would need the services of a man of such ability and prestige. It was expected, Robertson stated, that Davis could establish the justice of "incidental or consequential damages," even with the main mill several miles from the Great Smokies property. Albright had already talked with the chairmen of both Park Commissions, recommending that the Washington conference be held, as he had suggested in his letter to Davis.

Albright had asked that representatives of the two Park Commissions and the company come to the meeting "with power to act."

Strong Influence for Conservation

Damtoft, referring to his records, told the writer that the company's Smokemont mill, valued at $400,000, had been operated from May 1, 1920, through September 30, 1925, and that slightly over 9,000 acres of the company's park area land had been logged. Practically all of the remainder was in virgin forest, although "selective cutting" had been done in a small part of the lower elevations, before the company bought it.

During the September, 1958, conference Damtoft made an interesting statement to the effect that Champion Fibre Company had actually been a strong factor for conservation in the Great Smokies, although that had not been the objective. "The fact that the company had bought the unusually large tract, even with the intention of

COL. CHAPMAN. YOU AND HOAST.
ARE NOTFY LET THE COVE
PEOPL. ALONE. GET OUT GET
GONE. 40 M. LIMIT

—*Jim Thompson*

NOTES FROM CADES COVE: The attitude expressed in the grim warning sign, seen above, soon passed. Park visitors today find a pleasing mixture of scenic charm and "a page from pioneer life" in Cades Cove. Cable Mill, powered by the overshot water wheel, produces corn meal throughout the main travel season just as it did almost a century ago.

TRAILS OLD AND NEW: An infinite variety of views and flora may be enjoyed along the 500 miles of graded trails in the Great Smokies and along beaten footpaths of the park's wilderness areas. The path at left was used by Secretary Work's committee in 1924. The graded trails *(below)* were built by CCC boys.

—Jim Thompson

eventually cutting the timber from it, served to preserve it as a primeval forest," he said. "Had the company not bought it, to be held in reserve for future use, much of it would already have been cut by smaller companies that had owned it."

When asked for his current opinion of the Great Smoky Mountains National Park, the part he had played in its establishment, and his present attitude toward the park leaders with whom he had had so many conflicts, Mr. Robertson indicated that he is highly pleased with the way in which it was finally worked out. He wrote:

The program for the establishment of the Great Smoky Mountains National Park involved both economic and social problems that were difficult of solution and naturally stirred up animosities and differences of opinion that are now largely matters of history. . . . The "tumult and the shouting" has died long ago. . . . After the passage of thirty-three years those few of us who were active in the discussions can look back on the problems with greater objectivity and a truer perspective than would have been possible at closer range.

As president and executive officer primarily responsible for the handling of the Champion Fibre Company—later merged into the Champion Paper and Fibre Company—I carried a dual responsibility as the agent for the shareholders of Champion, and also as a North Carolina citizen interested in promoting the welfare of the community in which I lived. I endeavored to discharge both responsibilities in a spirit of fairness to all concerned. The situation, however, was complicated by the valuation problems that were necessarily involved, especially those that the lawyers placed in the category of "Remote" or "Consequential damages."

He stated that at the time the Canton mill was built it was generally accepted among paper makers that good paper for books and writing purposes, Champion's specialty, could not be made without a substantial percentage of spruce fibre. He pointed out that the availability of large quantities of spruce and balsam timber in North Carolina's Balsam Mountains and in the Great Smokies was a controlling factor in the location of the mill at Canton. Extensive purchases of spruce forests were then made not only for current needs but also for adequate reserves for an indefinite time. Champion, he explained, had purchased approximately 85 per cent of all spruce lands within a reasonable freight distance of Canton, 92 per cent of those holdings being in the Great Smokies. It was considered a "be-nevolent monopoly," he said, in that conservative, non-destructive methods were to be used in preference to the wasteful methods of logging that prevailed at the time—"Git, slash, and go."

Robertson recalled further:

As the proposed park embraced all of the spruce holdings of the... company, it was immediately faced with the problem of what to do about a mill that would be deprived of *all* of the raw material which made its original installation possible. Certain members of the park commission in-sisted that the lands should be valued as undeveloped forest lands without reference to the fact that the Champion railroad development had made the timber accessible and, therefore, more valuable; and that a mill which had cost more than a million dollars to build was wholly dependent on this spruce timber for its continued operation.

On the issue of "Remote" and "Consequential damages" it looked as though an "irresistible force had met an immovable object," and that a complete stalemate would prevail.

"Kicked into Prosperity"

But, he explained, after the sale to the park had been completed, the company's research scientists proceeded at greater speed with a series of tests to determine if any other woods native to the region could be made to serve as an alternate for the spruce fibres in mak-ing book and writing papers. Encouraging preliminary results were obtained from pine, as had also been done by other companies in making newsprint, but there was a vast difference between the nec-essary processing of the two kinds of wood. He said that continued experimental work, advancing step by step for a decade after the sale of the park land, finally resulted in a process that produced a qual-ity of paper, using pine fibres, that was fully acceptable to the paper-consuming public and at a cost that was satisfactory. "The costs of growing and harvesting pine timber, in the Piedmont, are without a doubt lower than the costs of growing and harvesting spruce in the Smokies would have been," he wrote. "In retrospect we could say that what we considered a disaster thirty years ago proved to be 'a cloud with a silver lining.' As it turned out, we were 'kicked into prosperity.' "

94

He pointed out, however, that the happy turn of events could not have been foreseen at the time of the sale. There was then no indication that a substitute for spruce could be found, and especially that it could actually turn out to be more profitable than spruce. Had the pine process proven to be impractical—and it was not developed to a provable stage until long after the sale was consummated— Champion would have had to close the Canton mill, as had been feared.

"Champion officials are happy in the fact that the Great Smoky Mountains National Park has become a recreational and inspirational center for all of eastern United States," Robertson concluded with pride. "It has far exceeded the fondest hopes of the most enthusiastic advocates of three decades ago. Such sacrifices as we were then making were amply justified by the great success of the park."

It is the opinion of the writer that, had Champion officials chosen to hold to the Sevierville verdict as a measure of value, it could, and most likely would, have wrecked the park movement. There just was not enough money to buy it on the basis of the values set by the three majority members of the jury of view. The company's final agreement to sell at less than half that rate was an act of cooperation and a tremendous help in the successful outcome of the movement.

CHAPTER 14

A GIFT FOR UNCLE SAM

WHILE the Champion negotiations were in process, considerable other land was bought on both sides of the state line. It was during this time, too, that the first of the Great Smokies lands were deeded to the federal government. In elaborate ceremonies on the roof of the Interior Department Building in Washington on February 20, 1930, the first deeds were presented to the government before a large delegation, which included the governors of Tennessee and North Carolina, the chairmen and other members of both Park Commissions, and National Park Service officials. Governor Henry Horton, of Tennessee, presented three separate deeds—one for each of the three Tennessee park counties—for a total of 100,176.63 acres that had been bought on the Tennessee side of the park. Governor Max O. Gardner, of North Carolina, presented two deeds for a total of 52,000 acres in that state. This combined acreage of 152,176.63 was turned over, of course, before the Champion purchase had been completed and while North Carolina buyers were still busy with several large purchases.

The importance of the delivery of these deeds for park lands was heralded by newspapers across the nation. It was through this ceremony that many people saw the first fruits of the long battle.

First Superintendent

Further visible evidence that the Great Smoky Mountains National Park was becoming a reality, at long last, was the June 20, 1930, announcement that Major J. Ross Eakin, then superintendent of Glacier National Park, in Montana, had been named to be the first superintendent for the Great Smokies. He arrived for a preliminary inspection on November 22 of that year, but his official duties began on January 16, 1931. He had been preceded by Rangers John T. Needham and Philip R. Hough. As was provided in the 1926 authorization bill passed by Congress, the park could be "established for protection and administration" as soon as at least 150,000 acres had been presented and accepted. The principal tasks of Superintendent Eakin and his small staff were to protect the area from fire and vandalism and to establish and enforce protective regulations. This meant prohibition of hunting, which had been practiced by park area residents and others "from time immemorial." No easy task faced the rangers, as they set out to change the habits of generations of independence-loving mountain people. It required a great deal of tact as well as diligence. At about this time, too, a rash of forest fires, especially along the borders, created new problems. Some were thought to have been deliberately set. The Tennessee Commission offered sizable rewards for information leading to arrests. Approximately 3,000 acres, in several small tracts, had been burned before the outbreaks could be stopped.

The first headquarters or "park office" was located in the Post Office Building at Maryville, Tennessee. A few months later it was moved to temporary quarters in Gatlinburg, where it remained until the present administration building, near Gatlinburg, was completed in January, 1940.

In the meantime, land buying was proceeding on a most active scale in both states. By July of 1930 the North Carolina Commission announced that it had bought 104,000 acres, including the 52,000 already transferred, and that another 122,000 was then under condemnation. With the exception of the Suncrest Lumber Company condemnation case, which was carried to the U. S. Supreme Court, the North Carolina Commission and its buyers did not have as much difficulty as did their colleagues in Tennessee, who had many condemnation suits, of which four were bitter and long-drawn-out court fights. On October 24, 1930, the North Carolina Commission announced that its work was nearing an end and that it was closing the field offices in Waynesville and Bryson City. The few remaining cases were handled from the main office in Asheville.

Six-Year Court Battle

One of the most troublesome and lengthy cases that had to be handled by the Tennessee Commission was the relatively small tract of 375 acres that belonged to John W. Oliver, in Cades Cove. Oliver, a great-grandson of the Cove's first permanent white settler, had refused to sell, and condemnation proceedings were filed against him in July, 1929. He won the first suit on the ground that the federal government had never actually said that Cades Cove was essential to the park. After the Secretary of the Interior officially announced that the Cove was necessary, another suit was filed. This case was in and out of court for a period of more than six years, including three times before the Tennessee Supreme Court.

The jury of view placed the value of the property at $10,650, after which Mr. Oliver won his first appeal to the Supreme Court, a request for a trial before a jury of twelve in circuit court. The jury of twelve awarded Mr. Oliver the sum of $17,000, plus interest of $700, whereupon he again appealed to the State Supreme Court, but that body refused any further review of the case.

Problems and side-issues of the Oliver case were out of all proportion to the small size of the tract. It had been expected that Mr. Oliver would be a local leader in the park work, but he developed an antagonistic attitude early in the land-buying efforts in the Cove. Mr. Oliver, a man of deep religious and moral convictions, bitterly resented the fact that a certain land-buyer who was personally objectionable to him had been assigned to work in the Cove. When members of the Park Commission saw that general opposition to this buyer had developed, he was withdrawn.

Opposition to the park continued, nevertheless, from several sources in the Cove. Colonel Chapman reported to the writer and others that he had received an anonymous telephone call warning him that, if he came into the Cove again, he would "spend the next night in hell." On a subsequent trip Chapman and companions found, and brought back, a crude home-made sign on an unpainted board, about three feet long and less than a foot wide, which bore the following message:

COL. CHAPMAN YOU AND HOAST ARE NOTFY LET THE COVE PEOPL ALONE. GET OUT. GET GONE. 40 M. LIMIT.

This unmistakable threat was nailed to a tree at the junction of the Rich Mountain Road and the "loop" road that girdles Cades Cove, near the Missionary Baptist Church. The "40 M. LIMIT" warning was interpreted not as a reference to a miles-per-hour speed limit, but as a way of telling the Colonel to come no closer than forty miles to Cades Cove—the distance between Knoxville and the Cove by the old route.

This sign could have been the work of any one of a great number of persons, as could the telephone call, for several living in the Cove had been bitter and numerous others, outsiders, had been sharply antagonistic over condemnations in and out of the Cove. It is not the writer's intention to point the finger of suspicion at any individual.

It is only natural that many persons living in Cades Cove and other sections of the Great Smokies foothills wished to remain there, and were more interested in doing so than in seeing the park established. In fact, it was recognition of this situation that prompted the Park Commissions to give such owners the option of selling outright at the full price of their land or at a somewhat reduced price and a lifetime lease. The establishment of a national park, like the building of a hydroelectric dam or other large-scale project, unavoidably imposes on a few for the benefit to the whole public. As already stated, no big public or utility project could be carried out without the right to condemn the property of some who do not want to sell.

"The Bees Swarmed"

In an effort to placate the relatively few residents of the picturesque Cove who had not already sold their farms to the park, Ben A. Morton went there and talked with them. Mr. Morton, one of Knoxville's wealthiest and most highly respected citizens and a stalwart in the park work, identified himself as the son of the late Dr. B. A. Morton, a beloved physician of Maryville who had a wide rural practice, including most of the people in the Cove.

Approaching one of the elderly residents, the father of a normal-sized family as mountain families of the day went, Mr. Morton drew, as usual, upon the local prestige of his physician father.

"So you're Doc Morton's boy, eh?" the patriarch queried.

"Yes, I am," Mr. Morton proudly admitted.

"Well, the bees swarmed ten times at my house, and your pappy was there every time," the old fellow confided.

As a result of Mr. Morton's peace-making mission and the tact and patience he used in talking with men, some of whom had been antagonistic, the new buyers found a much more receptive group of landowners, and many of them sold, some outright and some with lifetime leases retained.

Whole Region a Park

In the spring of 1930 Horace M. Albright, the relatively new director of the National Park Service, made his first visit to the Great Smokies—although he had been working most effectively on the project for some five years. That trip is doubtless still fresh in his mind for two unrelated reasons: the charm and beauty of the mountains in their spring garb and the rousing reception that he received in Knoxville en route.

Before leaving Washington for this visit he knew that he was to address a group of park enthusiasts in Knoxville. He was not, however, expecting such a throng as he found awaiting him at the University of Tennessee Cafeteria, where the meeting was held. Every civic club in the city canceled its regular meeting that week for one big get-together. The huge cafeteria was filled to overflowing, with a large number of cheering citizens standing around the edges of the room throughout the meeting. Obviously overwhelmed, Mr. Albright stated that he had never received such a warm welcome.

It is safe to assume that the enthusiastic greeting put the new national parks chief in a mood to enjoy to the full this initial visit to the park that he had been helping—and was still helping—to create.

On this first visit Mr. Albright was treated to a wonderful show of native white dogwoods. The countryside—both in the park and en route from Knoxville to Gatlinburg—was an almost endless array of brilliant bloom flanking the road and making fascinating borders between fields or meadows and adjoining woodlands. For contrast there were also the beautiful flowers of occasional redbuds and service (pronounced "sarvis") trees, and millions of small spring flowers. After several miles of such scenes, still some distance from the park boundaries, he exclaimed: "Dave, this whole section has the beauty of a national park." His companion and host was Colonel David C. Chapman.

That first trip was devoted to the more distinctive points on the Tennessee side of the park. In the autumn of the same year he returned for an equally intensive inspection of major attractions on the North Carolina side. This time it was a totally different phase of beauty that greeted him at every turn of the road or trail—the truly spectacular display of autumn colors. There were the yellows and golds of the hickories, sugar maples, yellow birches, tulip poplars, and many other species of trees. Intermingled were the various shades of reds—from intensely brilliant hues through the scarlets and maroons of the dogwoods, sourwoods, sumacs, red maples, black gums, sweet gums, and oaks, especially the scarlet oaks. Often these were set against a green background of pines, hemlocks, and spruce. It was as if that superb artist, Mother Nature, had playfully emptied her paint pots with reckless abandon across the mountainsides and wooded hills.

Best Time to See the Smokies

Today, as when Mr. Albright made his early visits, the floral shows of springtime and the autumnal extravaganzas are inspiring features of both sides of the Smokies. Persons who are even indirectly identified with these mountains are asked often what is the best time for a trip into them. A wide variety of answers may be gotten, depending upon the personal interest or preference of the informant. However, those who are most familiar with the rapidly changing moods and special attractions of these mountains find it impossible to name any *one best* time. Spring and fall especially, but to a considerable degree *all* times of the year, afford the visitor the rich rewards that stem from one of the most distinctive features of the area—the "unmatched variety of trees, shrubs and plants" that had been mentioned by the Southern Appalachian Committee.

Several years ago the writer set forth his answer to the question, and he has had no occasion to change it. Back of that answer is an experience of over three thousand miles of hiking and considerable picture-making done at all times of the year and under many conditions—the weather ranging from hot summer days to 20° below zero; the hiking, from trudging wearily along sun-scorched ridges—from which timber cutting and related forest fires had stripped the last vestige of shade—to pushing slowly through knee-deep snow. Most of this hiking, however, was through beautiful primeval forests. Back of the answer, too, is the knowledge that winter has some important advantages over summer for hiking. One of these is the wider vistas made possible by the winter defoliation; another is the fact that it is often easier to keep comfortable during winter than summer hikes. During the first few years of its activities the Smoky Mountains Hiking Club had many more participants on midwinter hikes than at any other time of the year.

What is the best time to see the Great Smokies? The answer of several years ago is equally true today:

The Great Smokies are always different, and always beautiful. Drifting clouds and the ever-changing play of light on the mountainsides are affected little by the change of seasons.

Summer or winter, there is a fascination about the dashing, splashing streams. The grandeur of cloud-piercing peaks knows no season. Alluring trails, winding lazily through virgin forests, beckon to nature-lovers throughout the year.

Many Great Smokies visitors think of these mountains mainly in connection with the flowering shrubs and the gay autumn colors. But the fairyland touches added by hoar-frost often excel any special summertime beauty. Flowering shrubs—rhododendron, mountain laurel and flame azalea—are special attractions, as are the riotous colors of autumn and the dazzling hoar-frosts of winter. But these added attractions have the same relation to the mountains that carefully selected jewels have to a beautiful girl. The jewels serve only to accentuate the greater beauty of the girl. Likewise, the special attractions of the Great Smokies merely emphasize the deeper beauty of the mountains themselves. The *real* beauty is in the girl and in the mountains—not in the ornaments they wear.

Yes, by all means, one should see the Great Smokies while the flowers are in bloom, when the autumn colors are at their glorious best, and when the hoar-frost and snow add their magic touches. But he will be cheating himself if he does not also go at other times—in fact, whenever he can. There is a rewarding beauty about the Great Smokies at all times.

CHAPTER 15

MORE DEEDS TO THE U. S.

ALTHOUGH there was not the fanfare that had attended the earlier deeding of park lands to the United States, the year 1931 saw an additional 135,705 acres transferred by the two Commissions to the government. In two separate 1931 transfers North Carolina deeded a total of 80,032 more acres, and Tennessee, in a single transfer, another 55,673 acres. Totals to date were thus brought to 132,032 acres for North Carolina and 155,849 for Tennessee—or a grand total of 287,881. The 1931 transfers included the superlative Champion Fibre tract. The main significance of these transfers is that they brought the park movement very close to the 300,000 acres set in the 1926 authorization bill as the minimum acreage to be secured before development work could start. National park officials had, however, made it known that the 300,000 acres was merely the legal "minimum," and that they intended to delay major development until the project was much more nearly completed.

In April, 1931, the Tennessee Commission had bought Cherokee Orchard, a 796-acre tract at the base of Mt. Le Conte, most of which contained an apple orchard and ornamental nursery, for $62,500 and a long lease. This may sound like a routine purchase, somewhat like going to the store and buying a dozen eggs. It was, on the contrary, a much more complicated and troublesome transaction than that. Principal owners of the Orchard had been among the leaders in the effort to exclude the orchard area from condemnation privileges in the 1927 appropriation bill and in the threat to fight the appropriation bill itself if necessary. Fearing the effect of this additional opposition, park leaders amended their own bill so as to keep the Orchard property out of the condemnation area. In 1929, however, the same opponents helped to prevent passage of a new bill to add this property and Elkmont to the condemnation area. The 1931 purchase, simple enough in itself, thus came after four years of controversy-ridden negotiations.

Another interesting purchase was announced in August of the same year. It was unique. It represented 1,020 separate "tracts." The purchase price, however, was only $2,000! What a bargain! Not necessarily so, because the total size was only 52 acres. The owner, Mrs. Kittie Carter, had sold large numbers of very small lots, she being the promoter who had given 25-foot lots to "winners" at a Knoxville motion picture house—in the hope that each winner would buy at least one or two additional lots so as to have room enough to build a summer cottage. These 1,020 lots were what was left of Mrs. Carter's real estate development near Wonderland Park, in the Elkmont section. Despite the small size of the whole tract, it required several weeks of negotiations to complete the purchase.

A delicate problem involving still another purchase was encountered in connection with the Orchard tract when, in the fall of 1930, the Methodist Episcopal Church bought 145 acres of land from Matt M. Whittle, one of the owners of Cherokee Orchard. This land, on Fighting Creek, in the Sugarland Valley, is just west— farther inside the park—of the spot that was later to be the site of the beautiful park headquarters building. The church intended to use it as an assembly ground for the Holston Conference. A Knoxville real estate man who was acting as agent for the Conference claimed that park officials had agreed that the site was not to be included in the park. Colonel Chapman emphatically denied any such agreement, and called attention to a letter he had written to a minister who was an official of the Conference. Considerable feeling developed on both sides of the argument, and recriminating charges of "bad faith" were made. The problem was resolved after many months of negotiations when the Park Commission exchanged land between Gatlinburg and Cherokee Orchard for the Fighting Creek property, the latter being recognized as much more important for park purposes. The Conference subsequently developed its much-used assembly ground on the Cherokee Orchard road site.

Condemnation Extension Sought

Having failed in 1927 and 1929 to get condemnation privileges for the Cherokee Orchard and Elkmont sections, the Tennessee Commission had another bill presented to the 1931 session of the legislature. This bill, however, had to deal with still another condemnation problem. The original privileges granted in the 1927 appropriation bill had limitations of both territory and time, the latter being a period of five years, expiring in 1932, before the next session of the legislature. This fact served to increase the opposition to the new bill, which sought to extend both the time and the territory.

The first official blow came when the House Judiciary Committee sent the bill back without recommendation. Such action often means the death of a measure. Next, the Senate postponed action until after the recess which the legislature was soon to take. Upon reconvening, however, the Senate passed the bill unanimously; but, in a delaying action, the House put it at the foot of its list for consideration and refused by a vote of 34 to 25 to suspend the rules so as to permit bringing it up ahead of its regular schedule. This meant the death of the bill insofar as the regular session was concerned.

Sessions of the Tennessee legislature are seldom dull, and this one was no exception. Austin Peay, Jr., son of the late governor, told with great emotion of having heard his father, in the early days of the park movement, assure mountain people that their lands would not be taken. In the heat of arguments a series of fist fights broke out on the floor of the House, and the aisles had to be cleared of legislators as well as spectators.

The regular 1931 session having adjourned without House action on the condemnation bill, park leaders urged Governor Horton to include it in the expected call for an extra session. There was no reference to the park in that call, however. The situation was desperate because, without the right to condemn land which was priced so high as to be out of reason, the Commission could not buy the land. Since it appeared that they might thus be left with troublesome "inholdings," park leaders felt utterly frustrated. A glimmer of hope soon appeared, however, when it became evident that a call for a second extra session was likely.

At this point pressure began to be "poured on" by park workers.

The *News-Sentinel* helped by running a full page of pictures and interviews with former park-area residents, who testified to the easier living on their newly acquired farms outside the Great Smokies. This time the efforts were successful and the condemnation bill was included in the call for the second extra session.

Now various forces renewed their efforts to get the bill passed. Mr. Cammerer, associate director of the National Park Service, sent a message urging this action and stating that it should make the park a "going concern" by July 1, 1932. Colonel Chapman told legislators that North Carolina would finish its land buying that year, but that Tennessee could never get through unless the condemnation bill was passed. "Even if we could get every owner to agree to sell at a fair price, we would still be stymied," he said. "Some of the land titles are so full of imperfections that they can be cleared up only through condemnation suits. Failure of the 1929 legislature to pass the bill has already increased land prices considerably."

To the pleasant surprise of workers, there was, in the end, relatively little opposition. The vote was 23 to 5 in the Senate and, three days later, 67 to 24 in the House. The bill, signed by Governor Horton on December 10, 1931, was regarded as a real victory and a wonderful Christmas present. Although it applied to only 1,366 acres of land not already covered, this action gave the right of condemnation in the whole park area until April 26, 1934—a little over two more years.

During this struggle for rights to condemn came the news that W. P. Davis had died on August 15, 1931, while in Boston. Although he was not on the Tennessee Commission and had ceased to appear in the forefront of park news of the period, up to the time of his fatal illness he had retained an active interest in the park movement, which he had launched in 1923–1924. Despite the excitement that attended the later work of Chapman and Morton, Davis was involved in most activities just as much, but more in the background. It would be a gross injustice to his memory to forget the tremendous importance of his earlier work and leadership at a time when others had had only a lukewarm interest or were not even on the scene. Except for the tedious pioneering of Mr. Davis, there would have been no movement in which the others were to do such heroic and vitally important work.

CHAPTER 16

CHANGES IN COMMISSIONS

WITH THE approaching expiration of the five-year terms for members of the Tennessee Commission, there were persistent rumors that another effort to oust Colonel Chapman as chairman was to be made. This time the tactics would be to seek appointment of new and different Commission members when terms of the original group expired. The previous effort, made in the 1929 legislature, had been to enlarge the Commission so that the new members could elect one of their number as chairman. When that effort failed, the anti-Chapman element kept silent, in the meantime possibly planning for his complete removal from the Commission. Circulation of the rumors brought a strong defense of Chapman's excellent work, made at a great personal sacrifice. Fears were expressed that his possible removal as chairman might endanger the remainder of the Rockefeller money, of which the colorful Chapman was one of the three trustees.

A front-page story in the *News-Sentinel* of August 21, 1932, included the following statements:

Efforts are being made within the administration at Nashville to replace a majority of the present members of the Tennessee Park Commission with new members who will supplant D. C. Chapman, more than anyone else responsible for the park, as chairman.

This is being done while Gov. Horton is ill. It is not believed he is a party to the deals that are being talked. . . .

George R. Dempster of Knoxville, former city manager and now [Tennessee] Commissioner of Finance and Taxation, is said to be the leader in the movement.

BIRTH OF A NATIONAL PARK

On the following day, August 22, the *News-Sentinel* contained this editorial comment: "Changes in the personnel of the Park Commission would be a political injustice to the seven members who ...have labored without compensation to bring the park project almost to completion."

Then, after pointing out that the Commission had been investigated and re-investigated—by the Rockefeller Memorial preliminary to the $5,000,000 gift and later by the legislature—the editorial continued: "Almost at the moment of completion it seems inconceivable that the Commission should again be subjected to the attacks of selfish interests who have lands to sell in the park area, friends to be favored, or personal malice to satisfy."

It should be noted, parenthetically, that, when Commission members and other park enthusiasts were waging an uphill battle to get funds, to get necessary legislation passed, and to push forward the multitudinous other details of the bitterly fought project, there was no great clamor for the privilege of carrying the load. But then (1932), with a substantial amount of the Rockefeller money still on hand, membership on the Park Commission became a sought-after position.

On August 25, 1932, the Governor's office announced the appointment of a new Commission on which Colonel Chapman and John M. Clark, the Blount County representative, were the only former members reappointed. New members were George R. Dempster and James A. Trent, of Knoxville; D. Clyde Bogart, of Sevierville; State Senator W. W. Craig of Ripley; and Davidson County Attorney General Richard M. Atkinson. These new members replaced Messrs. Morton, Conner, Allen, Colton, and Markham. Two days later Wallace Edwards, secretary to Governor Horton, sent a wire to members of the new Commission calling a meeting in the office of the Park Commission at Knoxville for August 27. At this meeting Trent was chosen as temporary chairman, after Dempster declined because he had to be out of the city so much. The new Commission voted to make an audit of the Commission's books and elected Ernest G. Heins as temporary secretary-treasurer, replacing Frederick A. Ault.

Two days later Trent cut the salaries of stenographers; fired Miss Marguerite Preston, whose work as office manager had won high praise from Rockefeller representatives; and named in her place R. B. Newman, who had done work for the old Commission as an engineer.

Officers and directors of the Smoky Mountains Hiking Club, loyal supporters of the park project from the beginning, held a special meeting a few days later and asked for the resignation of Trent as a member of the Hiking Club. Excerpts from the Club's letter follow:

> The Hiking Club is distressed that you accepted the temporary chairmanship of the newly-appointed park commission. . . .
>
> For what we consider to be your lapse of judgment we are not disposed to take issue with you at this time. But, your indifference to the feelings and your disregard for the past services of Col. Chapman, who because of the brilliance of his achievements, was long ago given an honorary membership in the Club, are such flagrant violations of the tenets of good sportsmanship that they cannot be overlooked.
>
> Because we feel this so keenly, we are herewith requesting your resignation as a member of the Hiking Club, and enclose herewith a check for $3.00, the amount of your yearly dues.[1]

The *News-Sentinel* for September 14 carried a report from Nashville that Governor Horton, in naming the new Commission, had insisted on Chapman's being retained as chairman.

In October Trent wrote a letter to the Great Smoky Mountains Conservation Association "ordering" the group not to issue any more checks and stating that the Park Commission was going to "take over" funds of the Association; and another, "ordering" the East Tennessee National Bank not to honor any checks that might be issued by the Association. At the next meeting of the Association's board of directors, a few days after receipt, the Trent letter was read.

"I move that the Association pay for our lunches and that the treasurer be ordered to issue a check therefor immediately," Mr. Morton said. His motion, made before anyone else had time to comment, was seconded by most of the other members, and the check was mailed that afternoon—and was honored by the bank.

---

[1] *Knoxville Journal,* September 2, 1932.

Trent, who had been an active member of the Hiking Club for several years, was quoted as stating that he had not paid any dues to the Club for that year.

Until then, it had been customary for members of the board to pay for their own lunches.

At that time, and up until November of 1939, the writer was an employee of the Conservation Association, with the duties of urging the payment of past-due pledges, writing articles about the park for magazines and newspapers, and aiding visiting writers for such publications. Another letter from Mr. Trent announced the "firing" of the writer. This letter was likewise ignored.

The Park Commission's request that the Conservation Association turn over all of its funds, then over $47,000, was also declined. In refusing to comply, the Association cited five reasons, as follows: (1) Both Mr. Albright and Mr. Cammerer had advised keeping funds of the two bodies separate. (2) Great Smoky Mountains, Inc., the North Carolina counterpart of the Conservation Association, had turned it funds over to the North Carolina Commission only to learn that it had made a mistake. (3) It was the Conservation Association that initiated the park project and obtained passage of both state and federal legislation. (4) Since its activities had led to the establishment of the park, it should continue with promotion and protection of the park. (5) There was need for an organization more flexible than the state-controlled Park Commission.

In November, 1932, Mr. Cammerer, chairman of the board of trustees of the Rockefeller Great Smokies fund, warned that the remaining $400,000 in that account might be held up because of "lack of harmony" in the Tennessee Commission.

On November 16, Trent fired W. R. Mize, the Commission's chief purchasing agent. The following week Mize was employed by the National Park Service to act as custodian for the land on the Tennessee side of the park and to handle the leasing of lands to former owners who had retained leases. After having received Trent's protest against the employment of Mize by the National Park Service, Director Albright highly praised the work of the former chief land-buyer and endorsed his new appointment. At the same time he praised the efficiency of Miss Preston, former office manager, and of Frederick Ault, former treasurer.

At the Commission's meeting of November 23, 1932, Dempster was elected chairman of the new Commission, succeeding Trent, who had been temporary chairman.

One of the last acts of the former Commission had been to file a condemnation bill against James B. Wright, chief park foe, seeking his Elkmont property, which had not been bought through negotiations because of great disagreement on its value. The bill, filed June 29, 1932, sought possession of approximately 330 acres of land, on which were a store, a filling station, several cabins, and Wright's own cottage. The case had been set for trial the following March.

Shortly after Dempster's election as chairman of the Commission he announced plans to obtain the Wright property and a few other Elkmont tracts through arbitration. The condemnation suit was withdrawn. When the arbitration board heard witnesses as to the value of the Wright property, witnesses for the park placed the value at from $18,020 to $18,427. The owner's witnesses placed it at from $138,940 to $149,180. The arbitration board (consisting of Major George L. Berry, president of International Printing and Pressmen's Union of America; Nathan Bachman, a former member of the Tennessee Supreme Court and later U. S. senator; and Sam E. Cleage, Knoxville clerk of the Tennessee Supreme Court) set the value at $71,000.

In Commission meetings there were numerous sharp arguments about prices to be paid for various tracts. At the meeting of December 12, 1932, a recommendation that $3,500 be paid to W. C. Garland and Jane Burchfield for their tract of 208 acres was rejected by a 3-to-3 tie vote. Commissioners Atkinson and Craig supported Colonel Chapman, who, according to one account, said that the property was valued (by appraisers for the former Tennessee Park Commission) at $2,000 and had been offered for $3,000. All Commissioners except Trent voted to reject the price of $7,300 offered for a Jane Burchfield tract of 184.3 acres. Chapman said she had once been willing to take $6,500. It was unanimously voted to reject $2,500 for the W. H. Ownby tract, for which, Chapman reported, Ownby had asked $2,000 previously and had been offered $1,365.[2]

Dempster-Chapman Fight

The ugly climax to the brief but turbulent life of the newly appointed Commission came on January 9, 1933, in the form of a fist

[2] *Knoxville Journal*, December 13, 1932.

fight between Colonel Chapman and Chairman Dempster. Chapman had presented to the meeting an audit report that had been prepared at his request, in which it was claimed that the new Commission had spent $11,067 during the previous three months but had bought only four-tenths of an acre of park land—besides closing purchases already arranged by the old Commission. Dempster's own account of the affair, as quoted in the *News-Sentinel* of January 10, 1933, was that, after the meeting had adjourned, he told the Colonel that whoever prepared that audit report was a damned liar; that Chapman then removed his glasses, hit him, and knocked him out of his chair. Then, he said, he got up and hit Chapman.

The fight was brief but apparently furious. The newspaper accounts described Colonel Chapman as having lost a front tooth and sustained two broken ribs, a blackened right eye, a bad cut on the lip, and severe body bruises. Mr. Dempster was not injured, according to the news stories.

This was by no means the only time at which the high-spirited park leader may have felt inclined to resist physically, or at least to express resentment against situations which confronted him. On several occasions he was subjected to personal abuse which he normally would have handled quite differently. It required a considerable amount of devotion to the park cause to influence him to ignore meekly some of the insults that were hurled at him by park foes who were in a position to hamper and endanger the progress of the movement.

For some time prior to the Chapman-Dempster fight public-spirited citizens interested in the park had been considering ways and means to take control away from new members of the Commission. A bill to accomplish this, by increasing the membership from seven to eleven, was introduced in the Senate by Senators A. J. Graves and Henry R. Bell. A similar bill was introduced in the House a few days later, but action was delayed by a recess taken by the legislature.

In the meantime park leaders were turning to a different method for dealing with the matter: that of abolishing the Commission and turning park matters over to a revived Tennessee Park and Forestry Commission of three members—one from each grand division of the state—with the governor as chairman. A supporter of this method was State Senator W. W. Craig, a member of the Commission that was then under fire.

An Associated Press dispatch concerning a meeting of the Commission held in Nashville appeared in the *News-Sentinel* of March 13, 1933, as follows:

Vigorous opposition to some of the prices being paid by the Tennessee Great Smoky Mountains Park Commission for land was voiced today at a park meeting by W. W. Craig, state senator from Lauderdale County and a member of the Commission. "Some of these prices shock my conscience," Craig told other members while several arbitration offers were being considered. . . . prices all out of reason have been paid. As a taxpayer," he continued, "I am having to pay for land up there that's being acquired by violations of the condemnation law." Richard M. Atkinson, of Nashville, was out of town, and pending his return only matters which Chairman George Dempster described as "routine" were considered. Among prices approved was approximately $72,000 for holdings of James B. Wright, in Sevier County.

As may be inferred from various proceedings, the influence of Colonel Chapman in park matters was still dominant, both in and out of Commission meetings, even though he had been officially deposed as chairman. And, in fact, despite an occasional outburst such as the one involving George Dempster, the Colonel continued to attend Commission meetings and to receive active support. The *News-Sentinel* editorial of January 10, for instance—the day following the fight—included the following defense:

When Col. D. C. Chapman struck George R. Dempster in the face yesterday he probably was not fighting the man so much as he was fighting stupid, dangerous politics. It was the last-ditch protest of a man whose repeated warnings have been ignored, whose advice and experience have been tossed overboard. It was the act of a man goaded to desperation by watching blunders upset a program which for five years has produced amazingly satisfactory results.

Commission Abolished

According to park leaders' plans, a bill to abolish the Park Commission and turn its duties over to the Tennessee Park and Forestry

Commission was introduced. It went through the necessary committees in quick order. It was passed by the Senate on March 28, 1933, by a vote of 29 to 3, and by the House on April 6 by a vote of 72 to 10, and was signed by Governor Hill McAlister.

Thus, the regime of the new Horton-appointed Commission came to an abrupt end in less than seven months.

The ease with which the bill went through came as a surprise to park leaders. The surprise did not last long, however. On May 11 Governor McAlister announced the appointment of George L. Berry, Pressmens Home; Charles J. Cullom, Mayor of Livingston; and Frank Rice, political leader of Memphis. Park workers had confidently expected that Colonel Chapman, Mr. Colton and Mr. Markham, former members of the Park and Forestry Commission— and all on the old Park Commission for the first five years of its life —would be reappointed. The fact that this was not the plan possibly accounts for some of the support which the bill had received from anti-Chapman men.

Harold M. Wimberly, young attorney of Knoxville, was named by the Governor as executive secretary.

The first meeting, attended by all members and by Governor McAlister, its official chairman, was held in the Commission's office in Knoxville on May 16, 1933. Since the new Commission had only about $110,000 in the bank and about $100,000 of Rockefeller money on which it could draw, it decided to concentrate on the purchase of the approximately 25 small "inholdings," about 2,500 acres total. Some 28,000 acres remained to be bought, it found, for which the estimated value ranged from $250,000 to $400,000. Thus, the Commission realized, certain small tracts that lay along the park border might need to be left out.

The *News-Sentinel* of May 24 contained the following statements:

In one of its first acts, the new Tennessee Park and Forestry Commission has voided one of the last acts of George R. Dempster as chairman of the abolished Smoky Mountains Park Commission, and thereby reduced by $3,000 the payment to the Morrier Sisters [at Elkmont]. The new Commission also cancelled leases of the three Morrier cabins to Mrs. Dempster, Clyde Bogart and L. D. Veal.... These facts were disclosed here today from records at the Park Commission office and through H. B. Lindsay, attorney for the Morriers. The leases were dated April 5, the day before Gov. McAlister signed the bill abolishing the old commission. They provided that the leasees were to pay $50 a year each for repairs on the cabins. The leases were for five years.

Among other cabin leases also voided was one to a Nashville political columnist who had waged bitter attacks on the Chapman-dominated Park Commission.

In a statement quoted by the *Knoxville Journal* on May 24, Mr. Dempster charged that the new Commission had lost $7,500 on its purchases of the 64-acre Morrier tract, with its three cabins, at the price of $18,000 and a lifetime lease. He said that his Commission had bought it, through an arbitration action, for $21,000, but with an agreement that, if the Morriers took a lifetime lease, the price was to be cut in half.

One of the first acts of Executive Secretary Wimberly was the re-employment of Miss Preston, who had been fired as office manager by Mr. Trent a few months earlier. She was made assistant secretary-treasurer. Mr. Wimberly had selected her, he announced, after receiving high praise of her ability from both Mr. Albright and Mr. Cammerer, of the National Park Service.

North Carolina Commission Also Replaced

Tennessee park leaders had had more than their share of obstructions and headaches, but theirs was no monopoly. In July of 1933 the North Carolina Commission headed by Senator Mark Squires was "let out," the route being by a legislative act abolishing the body. Its duties were transferred to a newly authorized commission of five. Governor J. C. B. Ehringhaus on July 19 announced the appointment of Will W. Neal, of Marion, as chairman. Other members were C. A. Cannon, of Concord; Senator John Aikin, of Hickory—succeeded in 1937 by Charles A. Webb, of Asheville; Thomas W. Raoul, of Biltmore Forest, treasurer; and Colonel Foster Hankins, of Lexington.

A condemnation suit filed by the old North Carolina Commission was still pending. In September, 1933, the Commission was considering an appeal from a jury verdict of $975,125 for the 32,000-

acre tract of the Ravensford Lumber Company. Since some 17,000 acres of the tract had already been cut over, Governor Ehringhaus said that he considered $150,000 to be a fair price. The company, however, had produced witnesses who said that it was worth $3,112,403. The company had been asking $1,400,000. State witnesses put the value at $600,000. Efforts to settle by arbitration did not materialize, and an appeal was taken to the Superior Court. On November 16, 1933, the Court awarded $1,057,190, which was accepted.

Thus the new North Carolina Commission had to start its career by paying considerably more than the estimated value of a large tract. Theirs, too, was to be a difficult task.

CHAPTER 17

FDR COMES TO THE RESCUE

IT HAD long since been obvious to leaders in both states that the money in hand would be far short of enough to complete the land buying, especially since land prices, in general, were rising steadily. U. S. senators and congressmen from both states were asked to urge President Franklin D. Roosevelt to allot the needed federal money from funds known to be at his disposal.

It was another of the real highlights of the whole movement when, on August 3, 1933, the President announced the allotment of $1,550,000 "to complete the project." Talk of a formal opening or dedication began. Secretary of the Interior Harold Ickes notified Governor McAlister that the United States was to start optioning and buying lands direct, rather than through the states. This announcement, however, applied only to the federal money. The two states were to continue buying with what funds they had, and did so. Another disappointment was experienced, however, when it was learned that the federal money could not be made available immediately because of an unexpected technicality, which was not cleared up until March 13, 1934.

The Tennessee Park and Forestry Commission had been buying small inholdings and by early August had settled for twenty more tracts at a cost of $30,000. With condemnation rights about to expire, on April 26, 1934—the last day for filing park condemnation suits under the 1931 bill—the Commission filed a suit against heirs of Morton Butler for the acquisition of their tract of 24,929 acres in Blount County, between Cades Cove and Gregory Bald. Since the Park and Forestry Commission then had only $11,800 left, State

Attorney General Roy Beeler was on the point of preventing the filing when he was assured by Mr. Cammerer that the National Park Service would pay the judgment.

The National Park Service decided, however, to handle the purchase of this tract in the U. S. District Court at Knoxville rather than through the state court at Maryville, and so a condemnation bill was filed in the federal court on October 15, 1934. The jury of view, appointed by Judge George C. Taylor, looked over the property and heard witnesses as to its value. Park witnesses placed it at from $394,090 to $500,000; one witness for the owners, at $1,414,712, and another, at $2,111,707.50. By previous agreement attorneys were not to "argue the case" before the jury of view.

In attacking the reliability of an expert witness for the owners, park attorneys sought permission to show that the same witness, in the earlier Champion Fibre case, had evaluated Champion's Tennessee land at $6,000,000, although it was subsequently bought for only $1,000,000. Such testimony was not permitted by Judge Taylor.

On May 4, 1935, four of the five-member jury of view submitted a majority verdict of $800,000. The fifth juror placed the value at $550,000. General James W. Cooper, chief attorney for the park, described the majority verdict as "outrageously high" and appealed the case to a jury of twelve.

When the appealed case was reopened on July 12 in federal court, with selection of jurors, any prospective juror who admitted liking or even knowing Colonel Chapman was challenged and thus kept off the jury by attorneys for the landowners. Much the same testimony was used before this jury of twelve as before the jury of view. Owners wanted the land and timber valued as of 1926, when the bill authorizing establishment of the park was passed. Park attorneys succeeded in having it valued as of October 15, 1934, date on which the condemnation bill was filed, thus taking advantage of the nationwide depression on land and timber values. Owners sought to show that the property contained valuable waterpower sites. This was refuted by a TVA hydraulic engineer.

The "Enormity" of $1,400,000

The jury's verdict, rendered August 7, 1935, after ten days of testimony, was for $483,500—not a great deal more than half the amount set earlier by the jury of view. Attorneys for the owners described the verdict as "grossly inadequate"; claimed that it indicated "passion, caprice and prejudice" on the part of jurors; [1] and asked for a new trial. They were especially critical of General Cooper's dramatization of "the enormity" of $1,400,000, the value placed by one of the witnesses. He had stretched dollar bills out on the railing before the jury box as he told the jurors that 1,400,000 one-dollar bills would reach from Knoxville to more than seventeen miles beyond Chattanooga—approximately 125 miles—or that they would cover an area of 144,000 square feet, and that the same number of silver dollars stacked one over the other would reach 10,833 feet into the air. Attorneys for the owners charged that such dramatics was an act of misconduct on the part of Cooper. [2]

The motion for a new trial was denied by Judge Taylor. The company's request for interest at the rate of $100 per day for the approximately 400 days from the filing of the suit was also denied, except from the date of the verdict. The $483,500, plus part of the interest, was paid August 6, 1937.

Colonel Chapman, citing it as evidence that the park had always sought to pay fair prices for land, remarked that the original Park Commission, of which he had been chairman, had offered a considerably higher amount for the Morton Butler land, but that it had been declined by the owners.

The same juries, the jury of view and the jury of twelve, which tried the Morton Butler case, at the same time tried four cases involving small inholdings within the Butler tract. Awards totalling $12,500 were given for the 453 acres involved.

Acreage Requirements Fulfilled at Last

With the exception of one tract of only 60 acres, the North Carolina Commission had completed its land buying in March of 1934 and had deeded all the land to the federal government in that year. In fact, most of it had been "bought" somewhat earlier, but the Commission had made only part payments on some large tracts. It was with money received from President Roosevelt's $1,550,000 that the

[1] *Knoxville Journal,* August 2, 1935.
[2] *Ibid.*

final payments were made so that deeds could be obtained and transferred.

The release of the 17,000 acres of additional land by the Little River Lumber Company, to which reference has already been made, brought the total of lands that had been purchased by the two Park Commissions up to 411,110 acres. Tennessee's final transfer of state-bought land came in May, 1936, when Executive Secretary Wimberly of the State Park and Forestry Commission announced the deeding of 18,739 acres. Completion of the Morton Butler purchase by the federal government raised the total to 448,000 acres. This complied with the highest acreage required to qualify for full development. At last the area was ready to be recognized as a real park in every respect except for the "full development" that was to follow.

Tennessee's Governor Gordon Browning, shortly after returning from a conference with President Roosevelt, released from the President a letter published in the *News-Sentinel* of August 3, 1937. This communication contained the following statements:

You asked me why the Government should not complete the program in Tennessee as it did in North Carolina. The sum of $1,550,000 was made available by the executive order after North Carolina had advised that $1,145,540.08 was necessary...and Tennessee advised that $858,828.64 would be required. [This made a total of $2,004,368.72. The remaining $506,557.86 of Rockefeller-donated funds, which at that time had not been matched, and the President's $1,550,000 brought the total then available up to $2,056,557.86—or slightly more than the estimated needs.]

The reliability of the estimates and the adequacy of funds were first questioned when court awards on the remaining North Carolina parcels were over $300,000 higher than the estimates. Checking the Tennessee estimates also found them far too low. The court awards in North Carolina, however, had to be paid to stop accrual of interest.

President Roosevelt then explained to Governor Browning that previous laws which had permitted acquisition with federal funds "for CCC and other purposes" had not been continued by Congress and that there was then no authority under which the President could allot further funds. Thus park authorities realized that it would be necessary to get any additional federal money for development through direct appropriation.

Congress Makes Appropriation

One sizable tract, that of the Aluminum Company of America, and approximately 100 small tracts along the border, remained to be bought on the Tennessee side. There were very few inholdings, but at least one of these was expected to be troublesome because of wide disagreement on valuation. The carefully made second estimate placed the needed amount at $743,265.29. Tennessee's senior senator, Kenneth D. McKellar, then acting chairman of the powerful Senate Appropriations Committee, reported having talked with President Roosevelt and having gotten the Chief Executive's aid in obtaining the needed money. McKellar introduced an amendment to an appropriation bill for a Western national park, providing for the appropriation of $743,265.29 for completing the land buying in the Great Smoky Mountains National Park. That bill, with the Great Smokies amendment, was passed by the Senate on August 11, 1937; but for fear of opposition which might have killed it in the House at that time, it was not presented there until the next session, when, on February 2, 1938, it was approved by a vote of 103 to 10. It was signed on February 14.

The pen used in the signing was sent to Colonel Chapman by President Roosevelt.

CHAPTER 18

LAND VALUES AND
MORE POLITICS

ORDINARILY a report on the effort of a senator to bring about the dismissal of the superintendent of a park would not belong in the story about the establishment of that park. Such an effort by Senator McKellar did, however, have a significant connection with how an important inholding in the Great Smokies was purchased.

As is readily understandable, the land which remained unbought by 1938 was some of the hardest to buy. The W. O. Whittle property, Junglebrook, between Gatlinburg and Cherokee Orchard, was in that category. It had not yet been bought because the asking price was several times greater than the buyers' appraisal. It had been left for later consideration while other settlements could be made more reasonably.

When the federal government took over the land-buying activities from the state, Whittle's attorney, General W. T. Kennerly, spent considerable time with Park Superintendent Eakin, during which he tried to get Eakin to recommend the purchase of the Whittle property at what park appraisers considered an exorbitant price. But, after failing, he apparently dropped the matter.

He only *apparently* dropped it, however. A smear campaign soon broke against Major Eakin. Senator McKellar sought to have him fired, basing his demand for dismissal on this charge, as quoted in the *Knoxville News-Sentinel* of January 1, 1939: "Eakin is from West Virginia and he's got a set-up of men from out of the state [of Tennessee] except two or three lower paid men. All of them are

Republicans but one or two. I think the superintendent should come from Tennessee."

The *Knoxville Journal*, a Republican newspaper which had usually supported McKellar, asked in an editorial headline for January 17: "Why Not a Park for Republicans?" It made facetious reference to the "seriousness" of McKellar's charge that Eakin was a West Virginian, but added that it was hardly fair to criticize a man for being born in the wrong state, and that, even if it were fair, Mr. Eakin could aver in his own defense that he had left it when the chance was presented to come to Tennessee. The editorial continued:

The second charge, that he [Eakin] is trying to make a Republican park out of it, is about the same thing as charging a man with murder and grand larceny combined. The assumption appears to be that under the New Deal no Republican, regardless of qualifications, has any place in the public service, even if it's a civil service job, as the park superintendent's is. We don't believe that Senator McKellar can get along, as the lawyers say, with these charges. There should be some solitary place, even if it's only a public park, where either a West Virginian or a Republican would be allowed to eke out an existence, protected by vast expanses of virgin forests typical of the Great Smokies; where, shielded from the scornful view of New Dealers, to have an opportunity to brood over their sorrowful plight.

In a brief special front-page editorial on January 18, the *News-Sentinel*, referring to the Senator's insistence that the park superintendent should be a Tennessean, asked: "Who are you to talk, Senator? Weren't you born in Alabama?"

Getting a bit closer to what apparently was really on his mind, McKellar was quoted the next day in the *News-Sentinel* as saying: "Having been in Tennessee only a short time he [Eakin] knows nothing of the value of lands in Tennessee. He's got no business passing on the value of lands acquired for the park." McKellar seemed to be ignoring the fact that Major Eakin relied on experienced land appraisers for determining those values. He was ignoring, too, the fact that half the park is in North Carolina—which should have given that state some voice in the matter of the superintendency.

This same January 19 issue also reported that Secretary Ickes had flatly refused to allow the dismissal of Eakin. "I wouldn't remove a man except for cause," he said, "and his political affiliation is not a cause; Eakin has done a good job."

The charges against Superintendent Eakin failed to accomplish their intended purpose, but McKellar and his principal advisors continued the fight. The next line of attack was to introduce this amendment to the pending approriation bill: "Provided that no part of this appropriation shall be available for the payment of the salary of the present superintendent of the Great Smoky Mountains National Park." It appeared for a while that the amendment would pass, despite the fact that Secretary Ickes had written a long and strong letter in Eakin's defense to Senator Carl Hayden (D., Ariz.), chairman of the Appropriations subcommittee, which was considering the bill.

Fearing that the letter had not been brought to the attention of other subcommittee members, the writer called Congressman J. Will Taylor and requested that he ascertain the status of the amendment. Although members of one house of Congress seldom interfere with matters pending in the other, Taylor went quickly to Senators Robert A. Taft (R., Ohio) and Arthur H. Vandenberg (R., Mich.) to ask their help for Eakin. Those two, in turn, asked Hayden if he had presented Ickes' letter to members of his subcommittee. Hayden admitted that he had not. At the insistence of Taft and Vandenberg he did get the letter and read it. The Senate then rejected the McKellar rider, which would have cost Eakin his job.[1] The vote was 31 to 28. In a letter to General Frank Maloney, Congressman Taylor gave full credit for the defeat of the anti-Eakin amendment to the telephone inquiry about Ickes' letter.

The *News-Sentinel* editorial of April 19 found hopeful signs in Secretary Ickes' stand on the matter and continued in the same vein:

Even more encouraging is the ... readiness of Secretary Ickes ... to join the battle to keep the National Park Service out of the filthy pockets of political patronage. The Park Service has as fine a reputation as any

[1] *Knoxville News-Sentinel,* April 17, 1939.

124

MRS. WILLIS P. DAVIS

"Mother of the Park"

WILLIS P. DAVIS

Started the movement

BEN A. MORTON

Powerful park worker

DR. E. C. BROOKS

Smoothed troubled waters

REUBEN B. ROBERTSON
Owned "the very heart of the park"

JOHN D. ROCKEFELLER, JR.
Saved the movement with $5,000,000

CHARLES A. WEBB
Influential park worker

W. B. TOWNSEND
Sold the first large tract

branch of government. This reputation is based on the reward and protection of meritorious employees and on that foundation alone. If McKellar is able to "get" Eakin it means that in the future Park Service executives will know that their jobs and their success do not depend upon how they serve the people but on whether they are able to win friends and influence people among the little ring of would-be political bosses. The Eakin fight is more than the fight to "get" or "save" one man. It is a symbol. Somewhere, sometime, the people are going to have to make a last-ditch stand against the political patronage monster.... We hope and believe that Harold Ickes is prepared to make a fight against the grand-pappy of all political pie-hunters, Kenneth D. McKellar.

New Accusations—CCC Funds

Those who were best acquainted with Senator McKellar knew that he never gave up in a fight. This trait was well illustrated in the Eakin case. His next charge was that the superintendent had mishandled funds for the Civilian Conservation Corps (CCC) camps that had been operated under his general supervision in the Great Smokies.

It should be recorded here, parenthetically, that at the peak of the CCC program—in the Smokies it came in 1934 and 1935—there were sixteen camps in operation in this park. Smaller numbers of camps were there prior to and following that period. At the peak, a total of 4,350 young men were busily engaged in building hiking and horseback trails, fire control roads, and a series of strategically located fire towers, and doing many other types of construction work. Most of the 500 miles of superb trails, which are now used by hikers and riders and are invaluable aids to rangers in the event of forest fires, were built by the CCC boys. Without this depression-born program it would probably have taken a score or more years to get all of these fine trails and other needed projects through regular year-to-year appropriations.

The charge that Superintendent Eakin had mishandled the CCC funds was quite serious and caused considerable concern among park friends. The Department of the Interior conducted a full investigation in the Smokies and surrounding regions. After diligently searching all possible sources of information, the investigators reported that there was no evidence of any mismanagement or fraud.

They found some accounting irregularities, but explained that because of the great speed with which the CCC camps had been sent to the Smokies, with inadequate provision for record-keeping, it would have been practically impossible to keep the records as would have been desired. They stated that money had merely been recorded in wrong places, not misused, and further explained that Eakin and his staff had done a remarkably good job in very trying circumstances.

Nevertheless, under the blistering fire of this attack, National Park Service officials sought to placate the belligerent senator. Consequently, in March, 1939, it was announced that Eakin was to be transferred to Shenandoah National Park, in Virginia, and that Superintendent Ralph J. Lassiter, the Shenandoah chief, would be sent to the Great Smokies. This brought sharp criticism from Eakin's many friends, including practically all who had helped to bring about the establishment of the Great Smoky Mountains National Park and Shenandoah enthusiasts as well. In less than three weeks the order was rescinded, and it was announced that Major Eakin was to keep his Great Smokies job.

Eakin's Ballot Smeared

An earlier incident, the most startling of the whole campaign, was yet to be made known. It came out on April 18, 1939, in a story which occupied half of the front page in the *News-Sentinel*. After a brief summarized introduction, the story quoted in full the letter that Secretary Ickes had sent to Senator Hayden, but which the latter had not given to other members of his committee until it was produced after repeated demands from Senators Taft and Vandenberg. After a list and refutation of the other charges against Major Eakin, as already recorded, the Ickes letter contained the following information which had not previously been made public:

According to sworn statements of D. Neal Adams, Clarence C. Corpening and J. Mayes, camp manager, senior clerk and clerk, respectively, for the Bureau of Public Roads . . . at Gatlinburg and Elkmont, Tennessee, they conspired to obtain information as to how Superintendent Eakin . . . and other employees of the park would vote in the 1936 election. The manner and method as to how this information was to be obtained was left to the discretion of J. Mayes, election officer at the Gatlinburg precinct.... Mr. Mayes stated that he marked the ballots of the park employees by ink smears from his finger tip and after they were counted he took them into his possession. These ballots were ... transmitted to Senator McKellar.

The letter went on to report Major Eakin's sworn statement that—after having been advised by a friend that the ballot smear was to be perpetrated—he had actually marked his ballot for Roosevelt and instead of folding it had placed it unfolded in front of the election officials. Ickes then concluded:

If the election officials saw fit to mark Mr. Eakin's ballot for identification, as is clearly indicated, it may well be wondered whether they might not also substitute a ballot.

From a careful consideration of all facts, I am convinced that there is no merit in any of the charges against Superintendent Eakin, and it is my desire that you and your committee may also understand the matter fully.

Park Officials Cleared of All Charges

Shortly after publication of the Ickes letter, Senator McKellar introduced a Senate resolution (S. Res. #131) asking for a probe of the charges contained in the letter. A few days later he introduced another resolution seeking an investigation of the Eakin vote. He accused Eakin of claiming to have voted for Roosevelt "to curry favor" with the Department of the Interior. The committee appointed to investigate McKellar's charges consisted of Senators Carl A. Hatch (D., N. M.), Gerald P. Nye (R., N. D.), and Henry F. Ashurst (D., Ariz.). In January, 1941, Senator Hatch reported, as had the Department of the Interior committee, that the investigators had found nothing to indicate that Superintendent Eakin or anyone else connected with the park had pocketed one penny. It did recommend, however, that certain changes be made in accounting methods.

Junglebrook Again

Now, back to the efforts to purchase Junglebrook, the 660-acre tract belonging to W. O. Whittle, efforts which had led to at least one of the charges hurled against Superintendent Eakin in the attempt to get him fired—the charge that Eakin did not know Tennessee land values. Whittle priced his tract at $200,000. Eakin had made it plain that $40,000 was a top valuation. With such a variance, the government filed condemnation proceedings as the only apparent means by which the purchase could be consummated.

Some witnesses for the owner testified to values up to $285,921, and all of them above $200,000. Values listed by park witnesses ranged from $14,487 to $22,600. Whittle offered to "donate" $40,000 to the park movement if the government would pay his price for the land and drop the condemnation suit. This was not considered, and the case was carried on with the result that four members of the jury of view placed the value at $70,000.92, with the fifth juror holding for only $50,025. Both sides appealed the case, and after several delays—during which James W. Cooper, chief attorney for the government, died—it came to trial before a jury of twelve in federal court. After much the same testimony as before, the jury on February 16, 1942, valued the land at $32,500 and the nursery stock at $4,200, a total of $36,700.

Thus, as had already been the result for the Morton Butler heirs, for W. O. Whittle the appeal from the jury-of-view verdict proved to be very costly, since the later jury gave an award far below that of the jury of view.

Land-Buying Completed

While litigation dragged on over a few comparatively small but politically involved holdings such as the Whittle acreage, the last really large tract was procured with relatively little effort. In November, 1939, a friendly condemnation suit was filed in federal court to buy the 16,288 acres belonging to the Aluminum Company of America. The company had agreed that it would not attack the constitutionality of the condemnation laws. In November, 1940, the Alcoa tract was bought at the compromise price of $220,000, which was very close to the government's appraisal. With the completion of negotiations over a few more small tracts on the then-established park border, the land-buying was at long last brought to a close.

Dedication of the Park

For many months park leaders of both states and National Park Service officials had been planning for a formal dedication. The crescent-shaped masonry wall and platform at Newfound Gap, the Rockefeller Memorial, was rushed to completion so that it would be ready for September 2, 1940, the big day set for the dedication ceremonies. A large bronze plaque placed on the masonry wall bore the following inscription:

FOR THE PERMANENT ENJOYMENT OF THE PEOPLE—This Park Was Given One-half By The Peoples And States Of North Carolina And Tennessee And By The United States Of America And One-half In Memory Of Laura Spelman Rockefeller By The Laura Spelman Rockefeller Memorial Founded By Her Husband John D. Rockefeller.

This memorial, half of which is in Tennessee and half in North Carolina, was financed by the two states.

President Roosevelt, flanked by political and park dignitaries from both states and by National Park Service officials, delivered the dedicatory address, in which he praised the functions of national parks and lauded the rare beauty of the Great Smokies.[2] The program was attended by thousands of citizens who packed into Newfound Gap ahead of the President's arrival, and was carried by radio over a nationwide hookup.

On September 30, 1940, George R. Dempster—for a few months the chairman of the Tennessee Park Commission—in his *Knoxville Journal* column "Like It or Not," included the following comments about the Great Smokies dedication:

As the President spoke atop the Smoky Mountains a few weeks ago, ten feet away to his right sat the senior senator from Tennessee, mute. Fifteen feet to the rear, beetle-browed unpurged Ross Eakin, capable Park superintendent. . . . Beneath the bronze [Rockefeller Memorial] plaque at the rear sat a famed Knoxvillian [Colonel Chapman], grown gray from wrangling funds from private and public sources to make his dream of

---

[2] The President had made an earlier visit, in 1936, largely because of an invitation from Great Smokies enthusiasts at the close of the Shenandoah dedication.

a Park in the Smokies come true. Able Arno B. Cammerer, former director of the National Park Service, told me in 1932 that David C. Chapman, alone, sold the park idea to the Rockefellers.[3]

Park Rangers Made Happy

There was still a rather serious and vexing problem, however, in connection with the boundaries within which park lands were to be bought. The line in the Hazel Creek and Eagle Creek watersheds, in the vicinity of Fontana, North Carolina, ran up to within a mile or so of the state border. The reason revolved around the fact that the owners of a copper mine near Fontana had held out for prices which, for park purposes, were exorbitant. Even though the mine, operated by a subsidiary of the Tennessee Copper Company, had been worked profitably when it was getting government subsidies, as in war periods, the prices asked at the time the lines were being drawn were far out of proportion to those paid for other lands.

Despite the fact that the illogical border thus created was on the North Carolina side of the park, the Great Smoky Mountains Conservation Association (which is financed entirely with contributions from Tennessee citizens and business firms) made vain efforts in 1940 to find some way by which the area between the park line and Little Tennessee River could be brought into the park. A letter asking for suggestions was sent to Mr. Cammerer—then a regional director, following his resignation as director of the National Park Service a few months earlier because of ill health. Cammerer replied in part:

In your letter of October 11 you put your finger on the one phase of the Great Smoky Mountains National Park that has bothered all of us from the start. . . . The North Carolina Commission and I had numerous conferences on the obvious desirability of rectifying the irregular boundary . . . but we found that the total asking price for the area . . . amounted to something like $23,000,000, due altogether to the alleged mineral (copper) deposits. . . . The acquisition of the area is highly desirable, but I haven't the slightest idea where the money to acquire it would come from.

[3] To clarify the point, it should be repeated that Mr. Cammerer himself first enlisted the interest of John D. Rockefeller, Jr., in the Great Smokies, although it was, indeed, Chapman who convinced him that the park movement was a sound and meritorious project.

The $23,000,000 asking price, an average of $500 per acre, it will be recognized, was almost twice the cost of the remainder of the park, although there were only 45,920 acres in it as compared to approximately 460,000 acres which had been bought. The land had no distinctive qualities but, because of its location, was needed to simplify administrative problems, especially to enforce fishing regulations, to prevent hunting, and to protect adjoining park land from possible fire, all of which would call for trails on that property. Rangers were practically helpless in the surrounding area. Dogs belonging to bear hunters could not know where the park lines were, and it was suspected that some of their owners did not care. The excluded lands were traversed by a narrow, crooked road—North Carolina Highway 288—which extended from Bryson City to Deals Gap.

National Park officials and park enthusiasts in general had just

THE FONTANA PROPERTY

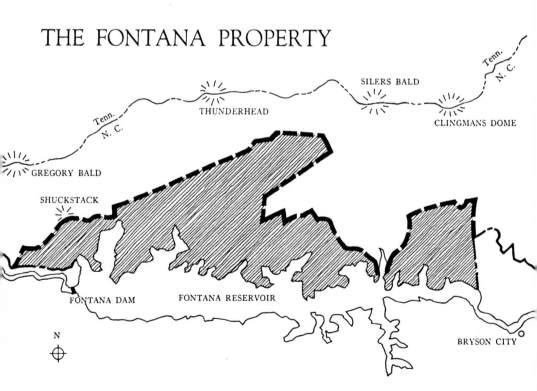

about resigned themselves to having that trouble-breeding situation as a permanent plague. The sudden solution, therefore, came somewhat like a bolt of benevolent lightning from a clear blue sky.

When the Tennessee Valley Authority decided, during World War II, to build the huge dam at Fontana, one of the first problems faced was the apparent necessity of rebuilding a major part of North Carolina Highway 288 because the backwaters from the dam were to flood it. The cost to relocate it was estimated at approximately $900,000. Cost was not the only problem, however. As is revealed in an official TVA report, the War Production Board had informally advised TVA that this road was not of sufficient importance to warrant allotment of the critically scarce materials and manpower necessary for rebuilding it.[4]

By a streak of good fortune TVA found a perfect solution—possibly the result of a suggestion from George D. Barnes, a member of the TVA land-buying staff. This plan called for TVA to buy most of the 45,920 acres lying between the park border and the high-water line of the future lake, thus requiring evacuation of all residents from the area. TVA would then give the land to the Great Smoky Mountains National Park in return for a commitment by the park that, when funds should be made available by Congress after the war emergency, the park would build a new road from Bryson City to Fontana. A modern road had already been finished from Fontana to Deals Gap. There were two other parties to the agreement, or contract: Swain County (N. C.), which had outstanding bonds in payment for the original road; and the North Carolina Highway Department.

Since the land was to cost only approximately $500,000, TVA was to save some $400,000 of the $900,000 estimated cost of then rebuilding the road. This $400,000 was to be turned over to the North Carolina Highway Department, as trustee for Swain County, to be applied toward the retirement of the outstanding bonds. Thus, Swain County was also to benefit from the gift.

The four-way contract was signed July 30, 1943. Congress passed a bill in 1944 authorizing the change in boundary, and thus this important 44,000 acres was brought into the park.

---

[4] *The Fontana Project,* TVA Technical Report No. 12 (1950), p. 475.

News of this transaction was received with great joy on all sides, with doubtless some special rejoicing by park rangers, who saw in it the removal of one of their worst potential problems.

One Inholding Remains

The public, including park enthusiasts in both states, did not realize, however, that there was still to be a considerable inholding —a tract of 1,920 acres belonging to the North Carolina Exploration Company, a subsidiary of the Tennessee Copper Company. TVA had paid the company $250,000 for flowage rights, including damages for flooding of the copper mine.[5] This, however, did not include the surface rights or any possible future mining activities at levels above Fontana Lake.

Preparatory to plans for building a road across the property of the Exploration Company—which was to be a park road, with no access points on the property—the government filed a condemnation suit in the U. S. District Court at Asheville in 1948. The litigation bogged down over the government's right, under existing laws, to condemn for a non-access road through the company's property. Nothing further has developed, although it is hoped and expected that this large inholding eventually will be added to the park.

[5] Letter from Park Superintendent Fred J. Overly, August 25, 1958.

133

CHAPTER 19

ENDOWMENT FOR THE FUTURE

THE National Park Service decided that the new road on the Tennessee side of the mountain, between Gatlinburg and Cosby (Tennessee Highway 73) should become the park border for most of the distance, and this boundary change was approved by Congress. The small amount of park-owned land that lay on the north side of this road was scheduled to be sold, and the privately owned land on the park side was to be bought and added to the park.

These border tracts and the 44,000 Fontana area acres received from TVA brought the 1959 Great Smokies area to 507,869.5 acres. In 1968 the total was listed at 512,655.01 acres. This increased acreage represents land bought by Tennessee for Foothills Parkway rights-of-way and thus is part of the park. By 1969 only 2,570.84 acres of "park land" were still in private ownership; when this is acquired the park will embrace 515,225.85 acres.[1] Most of the land still to be bought—1,920 acres—belongs to the North Carolina Exploration Company. It should be noted that the table on the next page includes acquisitions only through January of 1958.

Cost of Park Lands

How much did it cost to buy the park lands? This question is often asked. To mention only the amount of money would be very misleading. The actual cost includes untold days of labor by hundreds of dedicated and self-sacrificing workers. If it had been necessary to pay the leaders of the movement on the basis of what their

---

[1] January 1, 1968, issue of *National Parks & Landmarks*, p. 14.

time was worth to them and to their respective businesses, large amounts would have had to be added to the actual outlay of money. Then there was the $12,664,462 provided by private subscriptions, state appropriations, the Laura Spelman Rockefeller Memorial, and the federal government. Nevertheless, since the question of costs comes up so often, it may be of interest to see, in tabular form, just where the money that bought the Great Smokies came from, how much of the land was obtained with money from the various sources, and how the money was spent in each state.

LAND ACQUISITION INFORMATION [2]
Great Smoky Mountains National Park

Sources of Purchase Money	Acres in North Carolina	Cost
Federal Government	77,250 [3]	$ 2,161,930 [3]
Rockefeller Memorial	121,037	2,668,740
North Carolina	75,290	1,843,066 [4]
North Carolina Totals	273,577	$ 6,673,736

Sources of Purchase Money	Acres in Tennessee	Cost
Federal Government	60,920	$ 1,341,836
Rockefeller Memorial	95,450	2,396,260
Tennessee	77,707	2,252,630 [4]
Tennessee Totals	234,077	$ 5,990,726

Sources of Purchase Money	Acres in Both States	Cost
Federal Government	138,170	$ 3,503,766 [3]
Rockefeller Memorial	216,487	5,065,000
Both States	152,997	4,095,696 [4]
Totals, Both States	507,654	$12,664,462 [5]

[2] Information in this table was contained in a memo from Superintendent Edward A. Hummel on January 24, 1958.
[3] This includes the Fontana property bought by TVA and given to the park.
[4] This came from private subscriptions and state appropriations.
[5] The total cost, therefore, is slightly less than $25.00 per acre for the whole park.

All promotion and purchase expenses were paid from private subscriptions and state appropriations. All Rockefeller money was used for actual land payments. It should be noted that slight discrepancies in acreage figures and in amounts of purchase money, in comparison with figures given on other pages, stem from the fact that not all corresponding figures are given for the same dates.

What Money Really Bought

Just why was all that money and all that effort spent in establishing the Great Smoky Mountains National Park? It was to save the remaining virgin forests and the rugged mountains on which those forests grow for the enjoyment and inspiration of generations yet to come. Had the park not been created, there would have been very few virgin forests left in the Smokies at this time. But, with the park now a reality, visitors to this area throughout the years will be able to see trees and flowering plants just like those that were here when Columbus landed, and wild animals in abundance—bears, deer, wild turkeys, grouse and many others.

It was expected and hoped that many people would derive aesthetic rewards from their visits to the Great Smokies, just how many it was not known. On Mr. Albright's first visit, in 1930, he predicted that eventually there would be a million visits each year. Members of his large audience were not so optimistic. However, only eleven years later this number was reached. Only twenty-two years later it was doubled, and within twenty-eight years it was trebled. Since 1940 this park has consistently led all other national parks in the number of visits. It is the only one of the country's thirty-five superb national parks to have as many as 6,000,000 annually; in 1967, the peak year to date, 6,710,100 were recorded, with 6,667,100 in 1968.[6]

An occasional skeptic will claim that the location of the Great Smokies, close to large centers of population, is the major reason for the exceptionally large number of visitors each year. Such is not the case. Proximity to many large cities does help, of course, but that is only one of the factors. Shenandoah National Park, in Virginia, has the second highest yearly attendance. Shenandoah is still closer to

---

[6] See Appendix for further attendance information.

those centers of population; yet the Great Smokies regularly has a million more visitors than does the deservedly popular Shenandoah.

Why this phenomenal record? One need only turn to the official report of the Southern Appalachian National Park Committee in 1924 to find that the primary answer lies in the *combination* of the four distinctive features of the Smokies which that report emphasizes.[7] Let us look at them again and then analyze them. The committee, as the reader will remember, named these four features as especially significant: (1) "height of mountains"; (2) "depth of valleys"; (3) "ruggedness of the area"; and (4) "*unexampled variety* of trees, shrubs and plants."

On first thought it may appear that the "depth of valleys" is of no particular importance. But, after all—as Secretary Work's committee learned on Le Conte—to the observer the impressiveness of a mountain is its visible height above its immediate base, not the statistical fact of its height above sea level. For illustration, Gregory Bald, with an elevation of only 4,948 feet above sea level, is lower than the city of Denver, Colorado. Yet Gregory Bald is a sizable mountain, whereas Denver lies on the "high plains" at the foot of the nearby Rockies. And, as previously mentioned, Mt. Le Conte's elevation of 6,593 feet above sea level is not high as mountains go, but its height above its immediate base is noteworthy since it rises a mile and 21 feet—5,301 feet—above the park headquarters city of Gatlinburg, elevation 1,292 feet. By map measurement the summit of Le Conte is only five miles from Gatlinburg. No other mountain in eastern United States rises so steeply in five miles. In this sense, Mt. Le Conte is the "tallest" mountain east of the Mississippi River. It is interesting to note also that this is due as much to the depth of the valley as to the height of the mountain and that it is these two features combined which produce the third characteristic of the official description, the marked "ruggedness of the area." This ruggedness has an appeal of its own, but it in turn adds yet another superb quality to the Great Smokies—the charm and rare beauty of the crystal-clear mountain streams. There are very few level or nearly level spots in the 600 miles of trout-filled streams. They present an almost endless sequence of cascades and plunging water-

[7] See Chapter 3.

falls, which have their own strong appeal to nature lovers and trout fishermen alike.

Many visitors are surprised to learn how very rugged and steep these mountains really are. The fact that they are timber-clad to the highest tops tends to give the deceptive appearance of relatively gentle slopes. Here again, the combination of height of mountains and depth of valleys is of great importance, for it explains the amazing variety of the flora of the Smokies. Because of the one-mile rise in elevation and the resulting environmental differences, a visitor to the Smokies may make a trip of fifteen miles and find as many kinds of trees—130 native species—flowering shrubs and wildflowers as he could find in driving from the Smokies to the Canadian border; it has been said, in fact, that much of the rare charm of the Great Smokies comes from the Canadian-zone flora of the upper 1,000 feet of elevation. The park is, therefore, a veritable botanists' paradise.

The Park "Established" June 15, 1934

When was the Great Smoky Mountains National Park established? This is an oft-asked question, and one may get a variety of answers. For a few years the National Park Service, in its anniversary programs, observed May 22, thus commemorating President Coolidge's 1926 signing of the bill which authorized the establishment of this park. Some are inclined to use September 2, thus recognizing President Roosevelt's 1940 dedication. There is grist for a political party division here! The writer himself used to consider January 16, 1931, as the realistic date because that was the day on which Major J. Ross Eakin, the first superintendent, took over the protection and administration of the area. June 15, 1934, is, however, the official date. That is the date on which Congress authorized *full establishment,* for full development.

There is, of course, a distinction between official establishment and completion. Although this park has been officially established since 1934, it is not yet altogether completed, since there is a small amount of land still to be acquired, as already indicated. The 1,920 acres belonging to the North Carolina Exploration Company, the purchase of which is still pending, is the only important tract insofar as the public is concerned—the only tract that is holding up the building of much needed trails, fire-control roads, and possibly other facilities in the Fontana-Eagle Creek area. Except for this and a few small tracts still in private ownership, the park is virtually complete, and many millions of persons have already found education, relaxation, and refreshment of mind and spirit in the Great Smokies for many years.

After hearing a brief review of the host of difficulties in the long fight to make the park a reality, a new resident of the region said that he had once thought of Sir Winston Churchill's famous "blood, sweat and tears" only in terms of the vicissitudes of war, but that he is now convinced of the appropriateness of the phrase to the problems, disappointments, and heartaches of the movement to get a national park in the Great Smokies.

Role of the Newspapers

Much credit for the ultimate success and for removal of various obstacles along the way is due to the invaluable support given the project by newspapers of the park region. Without their active news and editorial assistance, the movement could not have succeeded.

There were brief periods, however, during which the major papers, one at a time, rendered something less than enthusiastic support. First it was the Asheville papers, the *Citizen* and the *Times,* that were "out of step." They were still campaigning for their first love, the Grandfather Mountain-Linville Gorge movement. But, when they did switch over to the Great Smokies, one could not have asked for more loyal or more effective work.

The *Knoxville Sentinel* was perhaps more consistent in backing up those who led the movement. At times, however, its support was little more than a mere "endorsement."

The *Knoxville News* fought with a zeal that is characteristic of a new publication trying to get established. Yet even this loyal publication went through its abortive "Conservation-with-an-Axe Association" campaign; but when it saw its own position to be quite unrealistic, even though idealistically right, it frankly admitted the mistake and gave a degree of support that was nothing short of inspired. It constantly went straight to the very heart of the problems of the day. Deeds of park foes were courageously branded for just what they were. This fearless and enthusiastic park support

139

continued after the *Sentinel* was bought by the *News* and, on November 21, 1926, merged as the *News-Sentinel*.

Throughout most of the long-fought campaign the *Knoxville Journal* gave splendid and constructive support. But for a brief period—under Luke Lea, then also publisher of the *Nashville Tennessean*—the *Journal* "dragged its feet." Although professing continued support, it backed the various efforts of park foes to oust Colonel Chapman as chairman—and even as a member—of the Park Commission, minimizing his importance to its leadership, stating that no one person was essential to the success of the work, and yet taking special pains to praise the labors of the many others connected with the project. It overlooked the fact that "the many others" had done their work under the inspired leadership and direction of Colonel Chapman and that seldom had a move been made without his guiding genius.

Importance of a Statement

It is difficult and often impossible to trace back to the very beginning of significant movements, activities, or projects. But not so with the Great Smoky Mountains National Park. This far-reaching project was started as the result of a simple question, asked by Mrs. Willis P. Davis. It reminds us that the oral word can be just as powerful as is "the pen." It was Mrs. Davis' voiced question—"Why can't we have a national park in the Great Smokies?"—which started this ultimately successful movement. Without it, there would have been no national park there today, and not even an effort to get one. Every step was a direct result of Mrs. Davis' question.

The millions of people who have enjoyed and are still enjoying the Great Smokies owe an everlasting debt of gratitude to Mrs. Davis and her husband, to Colonel David C. Chapman, Ben A. Morton, Frank Maloney, Governor Austin Peay, and many others for their tireless work on the Tennessee side of the mountains; to Senator Mark Squires, Dr. E. C. Brooks, Plato D. Ebbs, Horace Kephart, Congressman Zebulon Weaver, Charles A. Webb, and their many fellow-workers on the North Carolina side; to the officials of the National Park Service—especially Directors Stephen T. Mather, Horace M. Albright, and Arno B. Cammerer; and to John D. Rocke-

DEDICATION: President Franklin D. Roosevelt, standing with left foot in North Carolina and right foot in Tennessee, is here dedicating the Great Smoky Mountains National Park. The date is September 2, 1940. The place is Newfound Gap, site of the permanent Rockefeller Memorial. (Note bronze memorial plaque in masonry wall behind the President.)

—*Jim Thompson*

—Jim Thompson

TOP OF THE PARK: From the spiral ramp to the new observation tower on Cling-mans Dome (elevation 6,643 feet), we get a glimpse of Mt. Le Conte between the treetops. The tower is the highest point in the park.

BOTTOM OF THE PARK: The bridge at extreme left, on U. S. 129, crosses the low-est point in the park—the mouth of Abrams Creek which empties here into beautiful Chilhowee Lake at the western end of the Smokies. Elevation is 857 feet. At right, the unusual "rock fold" is one of the region's most remarkable geologic formations.

feller, Jr. The list could be expanded greatly, as it was a veritable army of dedicated and unselfish workers. But to list too many would tend to detract from the greater service and leadership of those named here.

Official Recognition

Official recognition has been given to seven men and one woman for the effective work that they did in bringing success to the Great Smokies movement. Lofty peaks and other important points in the park were named in their honor by the United States Board on Geographic Names. These points, their elevations and locations, and the park workers for whom they were named are as follows:

MT. CHAPMAN, elevation 6,340 feet, located on the main crest between Mt. Guyot and Mt. Sequoyah, named for Colonel David C. Chapman, of Knoxville, Tennessee.

MT. DAVIS, elevation 5,020 feet, located on the main crest between Silers Bald and Thunderhead, named for Willis P. Davis, of Knoxville, Tennessee.

DAVIS RIDGE, extending from Mt. Davis into the Tennessee side of the park, named for Mrs. Willis P. Davis, of Knoxville and Gatlinburg, Tennessee.

MT. KEPHART, elevation 6,200 feet, located on the main crest between Newfound Gap and Charlies Bunion, named for Horace Kephart, of Bryson City, North Carolina.

MALONEY POINT, elevation approximately 2,000 feet, on Tennessee Highway 73 a short distance east of Fighting Creek Gap, named for General Frank Maloney, of Knoxville, Tennessee.

MORTON OVERLOOK, elevation approximately 4,500 feet, on the Tennessee side of U. S. Highway 441 between the Upper Tunnel and Newfound Gap, named for Ben A. Morton, of Knoxville, Tennessee.

MT. SQUIRES, elevation 5,042 feet, located on the main crest between Thunderhead and Gregory Bald, named for Senator Mark Squires, of Lenoir, North Carolina.

WEBB OVERLOOK, elevation approximately 5,500 feet, on the Clingmans Dome Road between Collins Gap and Clingmans Overlook, named for Charles A. Webb, of Asheville, North Carolina.

Six of the eight leaders whose memory is thus perpetuated were honored posthumously. A precedent was established when Mt. Chapman and Mt. Kephart were named during the lifetime of the honorees. Both had the thrill of hiking to the respective lofty peaks which had been named for them. As a further tribute to the work of Colonel Chapman, the direct highway from Knoxville to Gatlinburg (U.S. 441) was named by the Tennessee legislature as Chapman Highway.

Yes, history was made in the establishment of the Great Smoky Mountains National Park. This park did not just happen! Nor was it created by an act of Congress or an executive order. It is today a happy reality resulting from an almost unbelievable amount of work by hundreds of faithful persons.

In retrospect some phases of the long and often bitter struggle seem more like nightmares. But there were some exceptionally sweet dreams, too. There were many times when the workers were in the depths of despair. What is more important is that there were other times when they were riding on clouds of ecstasy.

Mr. Davis did not live to see the full fruition of his work. Fortunately, however, Mrs. Davis, Colonel Chapman, Senator Squires, Mr. Rhoades, Mr. Morton, and others were able to taste the fruits of victory. Shortly before his death Colonel Chapman was asked this question: "If you could have known in advance what the problems and obstacles were to have been, what would you have charged as a fee to handle the job?"

"There isn't that much money!" was his emphatic reply, and doubtless a very true answer. "But," he added, "after I had gotten into the fight, I doubt if anything short of death or total disability could have caused me to quit."

Now that the struggle is over, we can see that the large number of challenges that the park leaders had to meet actually tend to add luster to their achievement and make it much more noteworthy. The fact that they had to solve so many annoying problems made the ultimate goal a bit sweeter and more highly prized. The obstacles are like the thorns and the completed park like the beautiful rose.

APPENDIX

Although the following information has no specific connection with the movement to establish a national park in the Great Smokies, it is hoped that it will be of some interest.

ATTENDANCE RECORDS

The highly varied attractions of the Great Smokies have drawn a steadily increasing flow of visitors, even before full establishment of the park. The only interruption has been that imposed by rigid travel restrictions during World War II. The estimated number of visits during the years for which records have been kept were as follows:

1941—1,310,010	1953—2,250,772	1965—5,954,900
1942— 728,706	1954—2,526,879	1966—6,466,000
1943— 383,116	1955—2,581,477	1967—6,710,100
1944— 534,586	1956—2,885,819	1968—6,667,200
1945— 750,690	1957—2,943,732	1969—6,331,100
1946—1,157,930	1958—3,168,944	1970—6,778,500
1947—1,204,017	1959—3,162,318	1971—7,179,000
1948—1,469,749	1960—4,528,587	1972—8,040,600
1949—1,539,641	1961—4,762,108	1973—7,892,100
1950—1,843,620	1962—5,209,803	1974—7,807,800
1951—1,945,100	1963—5,258,653	1975—8,541,500
1952—2,322,152	1964—5,321,100	1976—8,991,500

Of the thirty-seven national parks in 1976, only ten had as many as 2,500,000 estimated yearly visits. These ten, their locations, and their respective number of estimated visits in 1976 were:

Great Smoky Mountains (North Carolina and Tennessee) .8,991,500
Hot Springs (Arkansas) 4,737,600
Grand Teton (Wyoming) 3,856,800
Grand Canyon (Arizona) 3,026,200
Acadia (Maine) 2,775,100
Yosemite (California) 2,753,100
Rocky Mountain (Colorado) 2,741,400
Shenandoah (Virginia) 2,714,500
Olympic (Washington) 2,672,500
Yellowstone (Wyoming, Montana, Idaho) 2,525,200

SUPERINTENDENTS OF THE PARK

A total of nine superintendents and three acting superintendents
(indicated by asterisks) have guided the destinies of the Great Smoky
Mountains National Park. These officials, and their respective periods of
service, are as follows.

J. Ross Eakin, January 16, 1931—March 31, 1945
*John T. Needham, April 1, 1945—May 13, 1945
Blair A. Ross, May 14, 1945—December 31, 1949
*Robert P. White, January 1, 1950—September 15, 1951
John C. Preston, September 16, 1951—October 31, 1952
Edward A. Hummel, November 1, 1952—May 31, 1958
Fred J. Overly, June 1, 1958—May 31, 1963
*David deL. Condon, June 1, 1963—November 9, 1963
George W. Fry, November 10, 1963—July 12, 1969
Keith Neilson, July 13, 1969—June 12, 1971
Vincent Ellis, June 13, 1971—June 30, 1975
Boyd Evison, July 1, 1975—

THE FOOTHILLS PARKWAY

This 72-mile highly scenic parkway, which is roughly parallel to the
Tennessee border of Great Smoky Mountains National Park, was con-
ceived by the late General Frank Maloney while he was vice president
of the Great Smoky Mountains Conservation Association. The parkway
was promoted by him on behalf of the Association. He cited the fact that
the highway would facilitate travel between various sections of the park,
provide thrilling views not otherwise available, and offer excellent sites

for picnic areas and campgrounds. The original cost estimate was $15,000,000, but after long delays the estimate was raised to double that amount.

The rights-of-way were to be bought by the Tennessee Highway Department, and money for construction and maintenance was to be provided by Congress. In 1944 Congress passed the enabling act, and the Tennessee legislation was enacted in 1945.

Despite continuous prodding by the Conservation Association, one Tennessee governor after another turned a deaf ear on the project. The state's act merely *authorized,* but did not *direct,* the land purchase. Then, in 1956, Governor Frank Clement officially approved the project. There were, however, to be further delays caused by litigation over land titles.

Finally, on July 21, 1960 construction was started on the section from Little River, near Walland, westward along the slope of Chilhowee Mountain to scenic Look Rock and Murray Gap. This section was completed and opened for public use in September, 1965. From Murray Gap the construction continued westward to U. S. Highway 129 and the Little Tennessee River. This section, at the western end of the project, was opened for public use in 1966.

Construction then shifted to the eastern end of the parkway—from I-40 westward across Green Mountain and into Cosby, on State Highway 32. This was completed and opened for public use in 1968.

The only other construction to be started was from Little River, near Walland, eastward to Carr Creek. The grading and preliminary surfacing was completed in 1967, but, because of massive slides, the road has not yet (1977) been paved and therefore never has been opened to the public.

This leaves four sections of the parkway on which no construction has been started—thus only three of the designated eight sections are now in use. During the dormant period Congress did make two small appropriations—a year apart—but both were "frozen" before another construction project could be started. NPS officials are hopeful that the project can be revived "soon."

Boyd Evison, superintendent of the Great Smoky Mountains National Park, reported that the Tennessee Highway Department has bought all of the needed land and that titles for one section have been turned over to the government, but that titles to the other three sections are still being held by the state—awaiting assurance that money for construction is available.

Construction costs up to 1977 have been $14,300,000, Evison reported; he predicts that it reach a total of approximately $70,000,000. Inflation has been a major factor in the drastic increase in costs. If Congress had provided the construction money when needed, the over-all cost would have been much less.

The Tennessee Highway Department has spent approximately $6,000,000 for the rights-of-way and for engineering work. Unfortunately, much of this land—now off the tax rolls—has been lying idle for several years.

The lengths and locations of the eight sections of the Foothills Parkway are:

SECTION 8A—5.6 miles from Interstate 40, along Pigeon River, westward across picturesque Green Mountain to Cosby.

SECTION 8B—14.1 miles from Cosby along the south slope of Webb Mountain to Pittman Center.

SECTION 8C—9.6 miles from Pittman Center westward, north of Gatlinburg, to U. S. 441 near Pigeon Forge.

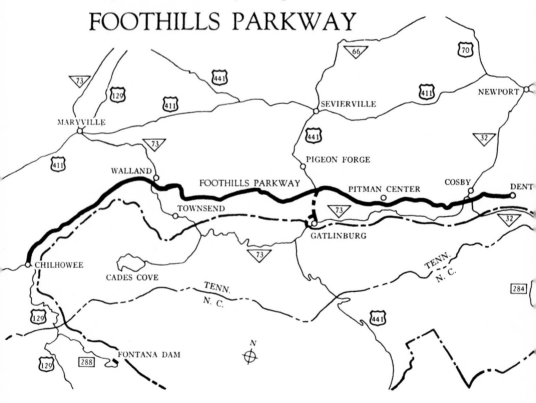

FOOTHILLS PARKWAY

SECTION 8D—9.8 miles from U. S. 441 westward along the north slope of Cove Mountain then across the west end of Wears Valley to a junction with the Wears Valley road.

SECTION 8E—9.7 miles from the Wears Valley road westward along the upper slope of dramatic Rocky Mountain then down to Carr Creek.

SECTION 8F—6.1 miles from Carr Creek westward to Little River and Tennessee Highway 73, near Walland.

SECTION 8G—10.1 miles from Tennessee Highway 73 westward along Chilhowee Mountain to Murray Gap, near spectacular Look Rock.

SECTION 8H—6.9 miles from Murray Gap westward to U. S. 129 and the Chilhowee Lake embayment of Little Tennessee River.

The GSM Conservation Association is still working to revive the Foothills Parkway project. Although discouraged by the ten-year dormant period, there is hope now that construction may be started again within the next year.

Even though it will be some years before this 72-mile project is completed, large numbers of visitors have been enjoying the completed portions. Master plans call for campgrounds, picnic areas, nature trails, and information stations at several points when the entire parkway is in use.

CADES COVE

For more than a decade the Conservation Association pleaded with park officials to keep Cades Cove as an open meadow, so as to provide the highly pleasing views of Thunderhead, Gregory Bald, Rich Mountain, and the wall of mountains that surrounds the cove. The pastoral charm of this secluded valley had already made it one of the major attractions in the Great Smokies. But, as farmer after farmer moved out, following the sale of his land to the park, the forests were rapidly encroaching and blotting out the views. The invariable answer was that the established park policy was to let nature take its course.

The happy solution came in a suggestion from a man who was later to become superintendent of the Great Smokies, but was then head of another park, Edward A. Hummel. It was his recommendation that Cades Cove be recognized as an historical area (which it really is) within a national park.

Although the idea was accepted in principle, there was still the problem of how to keep the rapidly growing pines from "taking over." The approved solution was to permit the grazing of beef cattle and the growing of hay crops for winter feed. That decision, announced in 1945, brought considerable rejoicing.

The old grist mill, built and operated in pre-park days by John P. Cable, is now operated from May through October each year. The water-ground corn meal which it produces is sold in the nearby store, as are books and other park-related items, including sorghum molasses, which is made at this location each autumn. These activities are operated by the GSM Natural History Association. Profits made by the Association are used in its interpretive program.

Great Smoky Mountains, Inc.

The Conservation Association's North Carolina counterpart, Great Smoky Mountains, Inc., had a relatively short but tremendously important existence. It raised almost $500,000 in pledges for money to be used in the promotion of the Great Smokies movement and to help buy the land. It also obtained the passage of the $2,000,000 appropriation bill in the 1927 session of the North Carolina legislature. Both were extremely difficult tasks, neither of which could have been accomplished without the tireless work of a dedicated group of men.

But, when the state appropriation was made and the North Carolina Park Commission was appointed, Great Smoky Mountains, Inc., considered its mission to have been completed and in the spring of 1927 disbanded after turning over to the Park Commission a substantial sum of money—all that remained.

In a report which he made to the North Carolina Park Commission in 1933 Verne Rhoades, executive secretary of the group, gave a summary of expenditures which had been made by Great Smoky Mountains, Inc., during the two years in which it functioned. Those expenditures, brought into major categories, were as follows:

Travel expenses	$ 1,470.26
Salaries	4,005.00
Advertising	4,517.58
Campaign promotion	31,684.53
Interest	175.00
Office expense	1,277.17
Total	$43,129.54

GREAT SMOKY MOUNTAINS CONSERVATION ASSOCIATION

As has already been reported, is was the Great Smoky Mountains Conservation Association, with offices located in Knoxville, that in 1924 started the successful movement for the establishment of a national park in the Great Smoky Mountains of North Carolina and Tennessee. For several years its entire efforts were devoted to the campaign for the park's establishment. But, as is shown on the organization's letterhead, it was "Organized to establish a national park . . . and to protect and promote its interest before and after completion."

As soon as it was seen that the park was assured, the Association became primarily concerned with protection and sane development. A bit later the organization's charter was amended to permit the activities to be broadened through ". . . financial assistance or otherwise advocating, fostering and furthering other projects germane to its best use and enjoyment as a national park . . . ."

In the field of protection, the Association vigorously and successfully opposed proposals of outside interests for projects that were wholly inconsistent with the purposes of national parks. Two such projects were (1) a tunnel under Chimney Tops, from which a vertical elevator shaft would have led to the summit; and (2) a chair lift from Cherokee Orchard to the top of Mt. Le Conte. Most of the activities, however, were focused on seeking increased Congressional appropriations for critically-needed additional park personnel, especially naturalists and rangers; and for such needed developments as the new observation tower on Clingmans Dome, new visitor centers, the Foothills Parkway, the highly-successful "Mission 66" program, and other forms of general support for the entire National Park Service.

In 1964 the Association submitted a list of sixteen specific recommendations for possible inclusion in the master plan for the Great Smokies. These recommendations represented weeks of detailed study by an Association Committee, with final approval of its Board of Directors. Park officials later complimented the Association for the thoroughness of its work and indicated general approval of nearly all of the items.

In 1965, with one negative vote and one member "not voting," the Board voted to endorse the proposed trans-mountain road from Bryson City to Townsend, with the understanding that it was to be in lieu of the Bryson City-Fontana Dam road which the National Park Service was contractually obligated to build.

Activities that were authorized by the amended charter include: (1) The expenditure of more than $1,000 for the purchase of file cabinets, many back issues of several scientific journals, and other items needed by the naturalist department but which could not be obtained through park appropriations; (2) A subsidy for writing the first edition of this book, and another to assist in its publication; (3) A substantial subsidy to permit greatly enlarging the first edition of GREAT SMOKY MOUNTAINS WILDFLOWERS so it could be sold at a price lower than total cost; (4) Substantial subsidies in 1969 to assure the publication of one new Great Smokies book and revised editions of two others. Total subsides have been in excess of $15,000. Each of these books will help visitors to get more enjoyment from their trips to the Great Smokies. The subsidies were granted to make it possible for The University of Tennessee Press, the publisher, to sell the books at lower prices, thus permitting more people to purchase copies.

Although the Conservation Association is a Tennessee organization, it consistently works for the best interest of the park as a whole—not just the Tennessee side. Since 1940 the Association has operated entirely without paid employees. Its activities are carried on by the volunteer efforts of a dedicated group of park enthusiasts.

In 1977 the officers, who constitute the Association's Executive Committee, were W. F. Moehlman, president; E. Guy Frizzell and John M. Smartt, vice presidents; Carlos C. Campbell, secretary; Dr. James T. Tanner, assistant secretary; Jo H. Anderson, Jr., treasurer; Richard Stair, Sr., assistant treasurer. Other members of the Board of Directors were Tutt S. Bradford, J. Kennedy Craig, David D. Dickey, Paul M. Fink, Ray Lee Jenkins, James G. Johnston, Samuel H. Keener III, Robert Killefer, W. L. Mills, Charles T. Rhyne, Jr., H. Paul Schroeder, Dr. A. J. Sharp, and Harold M. Wimberly, Sr.

INDEX

* Cities are listed only if official action was taken by the city.